'Authored by a compassionate writer who understands the darkness and abandonment of some of life's most difficult chapters, this book is a gently persuasive reminder of the power of myth—as medicine, catalyst, and, ultimately, as a way home.'

—Arundhathi Subramaniam, author of *Wild Women*

By the Same Author

The Inner Light:
A Beginner's Guide to Spirituality & Finding Peace

Table for One:
A Solo Living Manual for the Curious Indian Woman

The Monks Who Laughed When the Bumblebee Stung Me:
Discovering the Self through Chance Encounters

GOODBYE, I LOVE(D) YOU!

Timeless Indian Wisdom for Moving Past Heartbreak, Estrangement, and Quiet Grief

SUMAA TEKUR

HAY HOUSE

HAY HOUSE INDIA
New Delhi • London • Sydney
Carlsbad, California • New York City

Hay House Publishers (India) Pvt Ltd
Muskaan Complex, Plot No. 3, B-2, Vasant Kunj, New Delhi – 110070, India

Hay House LLC, P.O. Box 5100, Carlsbad, CA 92018-5100, USA
Hay House UK Ltd, 1st Floor, Crawford Corner, 91-93 Baker Street, London W1U 6QQ, UK
Hay House Australia Publishing Pty Ltd, 18/36 Ralph St., Alexandria NSW 2015, Australia

Email: contact@hayhouse.co.in
Website: www.hayhouse.co.in

First published by Hay House India, 2025
10 9 8 7 6 5 4 3 2 1

ISBN 978-93-6611-504-7 (Paperback)
ISBN 978-93-6611-629-7 (Ebook)

Printed at Replika Press Pvt. Ltd.

FSC www.fsc.org
MIX
Paper | Supporting responsible forestry
FSC™ C016779

Hay House is committed to a sustainable future for our business, our readers and our planet. This book is made from Forest Stewardship Council® certified paper.

To Janice,
the wise dog I fell in love with
in a South Indian coffee plantation.
You ran free into another realm, leaving me with lessons
about love and letting go that no human could ever teach.

Contents

Introduction

What Happens after the End?

A few years ago, I found myself sitting quietly on the floor of my living room, staring at a suitcase. It was half-packed. Shirts folded with mechanical precision, a toothbrush tucked neatly into a pouch, shoes carefully wrapped in cloth bags. But they weren't my things. I was packing for someone else to leave.

And yet, I couldn't bring myself to close the suitcase. Not because I wasn't ready for them to go, but because I wasn't sure if I was ready for the leaving to be real. I sat there for hours, my hand resting on the zipper, as if closing that suitcase would seal a decision I hadn't yet made. Was it truly over? Had I done everything I could? Was there still hope, or was I only holding on to a future I had imagined?

That night, they left. I stayed. But something in me quietly accepted what I had refused to see for months: This relationship, as I knew it, was no longer working. It's a moment so many of us find ourselves in. Sometimes it's a partner, sometimes a friend, a parent, or even a sibling. We realise that something has broken. And no matter how tightly we hold the pieces together, they no longer fit the way they once did.

What do we do with that realisation? Where do we go from there? That is the question at the heart of this book.

Why I Wrote This Book

If you scan the bookshelves, there's no shortage of books on relationships. How to find one. How to fix one. How to keep one. There are endless strategies for communication, compatibility, and compromise. But I found very few conversations about *what happens when the relationship ends*—or worse, when it's falling apart and you're still in it, unsure of what to do.

Most of us are taught how to begin things. How to fall in love. How to build a family. How to make friends. We also learn, along the way, how to make things work and keep them going, for better or for worse. But very few of us are taught how to end things. How to walk away with grace. How to sit with grief without losing ourselves. How to heal without becoming hard.

This book was born from my own questions, and the questions I heard echoed in the lives of people around me—clients, friends, family, and strangers who shared their stories. It's a book I wish I had when I was sitting next to that suitcase. Not a manual. Not a checklist. But a companion.

Why It Matters Today

We live in a time of instant connections and goodbyes. Relationships, no matter how deep or long-standing, are slipping through our fingers faster than ever. Divorce rates are climbing, families are growing distant, and friendships are dissolving over a single misunderstanding. We are quicker to start over, but slower to heal.

Technology has brought us closer, yet somehow, we are lonelier. We have more choices than ever before, and yet many of us feel adrift, wondering why love seems harder, why bonds feel more fragile, and why we struggle to trust. The old rules don't seem to apply anymore. But the ache we feel at the end of a relationship? That hasn't changed.

What has changed is *how* we approach that ache. And that's why this book matters now. Because endings are no longer rare; they are inevitable. But how we meet them can make all the difference to the quality of our life and relationships.

What Makes This Book Different

We find plenty of advice out there on healing from a break-up or cutting ties with toxic people. Some offer archetypes for better understanding, while others provide steps and stages. But I wanted to create something different. Something slower and more reflective. A book that doesn't tell you what to do but sits beside you while you figure it out.

This is not a book that pushes you to move on. It's not here to tell you that 'time heals all wounds' or to rush you towards self-love and positivity. Instead, it gently asks you: 'What do you need right now? What hurts the most? What's still unspoken?' And it walks with you as you answer these questions in all honesty.

I also wanted to offer a uniquely Indian lens to these universal experiences. In our stories, myths and spiritual teachings, there is a deep well of wisdom about love, longing, loss and letting go. Our ancestors have navigated these questions long before we arrived. Whether it's through the fire ceremonies in the Ramayana, the soul ties in Meera's devotion, or the karmic entanglements addressed in ancient texts—there is guidance here that's timeless, if only we pause to listen.

This book blends those ancient truths with contemporary psychology, real-life stories, and the rawness of lived experience. It's not about following a single path, but about showing you the many paths that exist so you can choose your own.

Who This Book Is For

This book is for anyone standing at the edge of an ending. Whether you're mourning a break-up, questioning a marriage, grieving a friendship, or creating distance from family, these pages are for you.

It's for the person who's tired of pretending she is fine; for the one who's reading all the self-help but still feeling stuck; for the one who has done 'all the work' and wonders why it still hurts; and for those who want to understand the deeper patterns, karmic loops, and spiritual lessons beneath the surface.

And it's for those who are ready to begin again but aren't sure how.

My Goal with This Book

If I had to distil it into one sentence, it would be this: I want you to know you are not alone.

This book doesn't claim to have all the answers. What it offers is company, clarity, and comfort. It gives you options when you feel trapped. It offers stories that help you see yourself. It holds space for your grief, and for your hope.

You will find reflections here, and questions that don't always have easy answers. You will find ancient stories that mirror your current dilemmas. You will find rituals, practices, and tools to help you heal in ways that feel authentic to you.

Most of all, I hope this book gives you the courage to trust your own timing. To move through endings at your own pace. To believe in new beginnings, not because you are forced to, but because you are ready.

An ending is not the opposite of a beginning. It is part of it. If you can remember, you will walk through every ending with more grace and every beginning with more trust.

1

The First Step to Healing: Acknowledgement

Roopesh is a 55-year-old divorced father of two who started a romantic relationship with a woman in his neighbourhood. Evening walks within the colony led to lengthy chats. Coffee dates turned into a bond that the two could not ignore. However, given that Roopesh had been burned in relationships before, he was reluctant to dive into a commitment. Yet, his style of relating to people was marked by warmth and deep affection. At times, he seemed to be transactional, and at other times, sentimental. His emotion-driven actions belied his logic-filled words, leaving the woman confused and wondering which part of him to believe.

She waited for a few months, but when Roopesh made no move to deepen the relationship or even indicate exclusivity, she emotionally disengaged. She still demanded her needs, asking with a deep sense of right for anything she wanted from him: Time, attention, dinners, and presents. But she was aware that there was no future in the relationship.

Roopesh sensed a shift in the dynamic but could not put a finger on it. His intuition missed the woman's openness, but he didn't want to bring up that observation to his full consciousness, let alone address it. Meanwhile, he continued with his interactions with her, having set certain boundaries that were comfortable to him. He believed that those same boundaries were acceptable to the woman, too.

He thought that he had the best of everything: Her attention and presence without the responsibility of commitment. He received all the benefits of a romantic partner without fulfilling any of the obligations. He did notice the emotional distance and disconnection but didn't want to think about it too closely. He brushed it aside in favour of continuing to spend time with her. He noticed the absence of excitement in her voice when he called her, and the long silences when she buried her face behind the menu card at the restaurant. He knew well that he was the one initiating contact every single day. It surprised him that she often forgot the things that were important to him: His travel dates and important occasions, but he put that down to her being busy and that it was a minor detail in a relationship that he shouldn't fuss over. He ignored it and continued. As long as he still had access to her, and as long as she continued to respond to his calls and texts, Roopesh believed that all was well.

The daily actions, such as calling, texting, weekend dates, attending concerts and long brunches, were so integrated into routine that he did not even notice the lack of spice and excitement that had first brought the two together. The relationship had deteriorated and was now merely transactional. The woman, already disappointed by what she could not get, was biding her time and continued being with Roopesh, knowing that it was only a matter of time before she moved on.

This has a new term in the modern dating world: Quiet quitting. This term is also used in corporate offices where employees do the bare minimum required to keep their jobs without being too emotionally invested in their work. In a personal relationship, much like in a work set-up, quiet quitting becomes a self-protection mechanism, reducing intimacy to a calculation of costs and benefits. It is a way to feel in charge of the story, to stay in control, and to believe the exchange is fair.

Roopesh, on the other hand, was so accustomed to her presence that it was more a habit that needed to be perpetuated. Her presence was much like furniture that stays too long in the corner of the room that you would miss only if it were gone, but you would do little to appreciate its presence.

The time came when the woman was ready to move on. She had found a man who was willing to give her everything she wanted, neatly wrapped in the promise of marriage. When she finally left, Roopesh was hit by a storm that only self-reflection could quell. He didn't want to 'over-give', but he also didn't want to lose the benefits of having her in his life. And now, he paid the very price he had tried to avoid all along. Looking back, Roopesh could see the moments when he had picked up the phone out of habit more than out of an earnest desire to hear her voice. He was on autopilot, blind to the nuances that revealed the truth sooner rather than later.

Recognising when a relationship is not working is the first step to preventing excessive damage from heartbreak. It calls for strength and expanded awareness. With clarity, we can identify the choices before us and choose the path that most resonates with our deeper purpose. Yet, often, even when we sense the truth, we don't want to see it, carrying on as though all systems are in order. Avoidance is only one sign of a broken relationship. Many other signs also indicate a broken relationship.

SIGNS A RELATIONSHIP HAS STOPPED WORKING

It is rather rare, almost impossible, to find relationships that have not gone through some rough and tumble.

Besides relating to people around us, we are each constantly undergoing change, growth, and transformation in both small and significant ways. We constantly relate to people as we go through these various changes within ourselves.

Our own transformations have a deep impact on our relationships. Every stage of a relationship, therefore, is one of growth, whether we recognise it as such or not. This applies to every type of relationship: Romantic, parent-child, siblings, friends, co-workers, neighbours, and so on.

Recognising that a relationship is not working is important because it makes us aware of the choices before us. But are we aware enough to identify, and then accept, that a relationship is not working?

Emotional and Psychological Impact

The deeper the connection, the sharper the pain of realising that the relationship is not working. How our body and mind respond to this insight often reveals the status of our mental health.

When a relationship falters, our acknowledgement of its failing status can be complex. Rarely do we ever sit and tell ourselves or a best friend that the relationship is crumbling. Instead, we rely on the coping mechanisms that we often go to when something is not working. The patterns repeat in every situation and in every type of relationship.

So, how do we acknowledge that a relationship is not working? Below are a few common strategies that we use—consciously or unconsciously—to cope with the realisation that a relationship is not working. All of these have roots in how we were treated in childhood and how we learnt to cope with the lack, or abundance, of something in our lives.

Let's examine these types, which would be all too familiar to you if you ever paid attention to how people behave when they get uncomfortable.

The first three (avoidance, denial, and distraction-seeking) are low-intensity strategies. The next three (emotional manipulation, anger, and self-blame) are medium-intensity strategies, and the third set (heightened fear, self-awareness, and rebound relationships) are either panic-driven responses or make for mature processing.

1. Avoidance: The Delulu Bubble

When confronting problems seems too overwhelming, some of us choose to avoid them altogether. This is much like the delulu stars, who glide through life in a transparent bubble. Inside the bubble, life is filled with unicorns, stardust, twinkling lights, multi-tier cakes, confetti, gurgles of laughter and the scent of roses.

Getting out of the delulu bubble is too painful, and some even deem it unnecessary. But when life flings a curveball at you, would you have the strength and the resources to take care of yourself? That is the fundamental question.

We often choose avoidance based on the nature of the relationship. In a relationship with a coworker who is not that important, if their style of communication is bothering you, you may choose not to address it, as it is too much trouble, or out of fear that it might spoil the current equation. You may simply continue working in the same manner to not upset the cart. This is technically avoidance because even with awareness of the issue, you hold back from addressing it.

In some other types of relationships, you might notice an issue but genuinely feel it is too small to be worth your time or effort. In such cases, it is not strictly avoidance but a conscious choice to let go of a minor irritation in a less-valuable relationship. In the really important relationships, however, you may feel overwhelmed by the possible outcome of bringing up the issue. So, you run away! This running away can take one of two forms.

a. **Emotional withdrawal:** Here, we sidestep difficult conversations and reduce emotional investment in a relationship. It is much like Roopesh's woman-friend's decision to keep things going for the sake of convenience while quietly withdrawing her emotions from the equation. This is not always apparent because everything seems fine on the surface. Unless the person who is emotionally withdrawing mentions something or leaves clues, this form of avoidance almost goes undetected.

b. **Physical absence:** In this, we find excuses not to spend more time with the partner. This is clearly visible and easy to detect. It is the most obvious form of avoidance.

Ghosting: A subset of avoidance is the act of simply disappearing from a person's life by abruptly stopping all communication. In 21st-century dating parlance, it is called ghosting and has been increasingly gaining prominence as an 'effective' way to avoid awkward conversations and protect one's peace. Many Gen Z-ers advocate this form of relationship closure. But mental health professionals hold that it is a form of abuse where you are not offering the other person the decency of closure. Ghosting happens when a person suddenly stops responding to texts and calls, hoping that the other will understand it's over. The term ghosting came from the idea that the person becomes a ghost, as though disappeared into the dead of night. It is believed that people 'ghost' others only in the initial stages of dating when they have met someone a few times and have decided not to pursue the connection. But ghosting can happen in relationships of any length and intensity, even marriages where one partner simply ups and leaves. Ghosting is not new. It has existed for centuries, but in today's world of abundant communication tools, it lays bare not a lack of resources but a lack of basic courtesy and respect for the other person.

2. Denial: La-La Land

Then, there's the denial that anything is wrong at all. This is quite common in homes where everyone's conditioned to maintain the happy-family facade, meeting their best potential and living their best life. To accept that a problem exists means that it would need to be addressed, while denying it means that everyone can continue living in their make-believe world, downplaying issues as 'nothing serious' and maintaining routine to appear normal.

This form of acknowledgement of a problem within the relationship is different from avoidance. When we avoid something, we still acknowledge that there is a problem and that we are not ready to address it. With denial, we don't accept that there's a problem. So, there is no question of avoiding anything because there is nothing to avoid or address.

Families that have grown up surrounded by rivals—whether with parents' siblings, neighbours, or anyone they felt the need to outdo—are often the ones most likely to deny when a relationship isn't working. This tendency then repeats itself in every relationship pursued by members of such families. They would rather deny there's a problem than go through the trouble of addressing it.

3. Distraction-Seeking: Busy, but Empty

This is another form of avoidance—seeking something (anything) to avoid confronting the problem. We seek distraction by spending longer hours at work or by diving into solving a problem that doesn't demand excavating difficult emotions. Basically, we want to take charge of an area of life that assures us we are in control, and we know how to manage things. Working longer hours also ensures that the person can be physically (and emotionally) absent from the stress-filled relationships. Deniers also tend to spend more time on hobbies to dodge the cause of stress, offering recreation and a sense of accomplishment. The hobby gives them a clear pathway to completion and success.

This is all pursued with the hope of never having to address the issue or relationship that is problematic.

For instance, if a marriage is deteriorating and the husband wants to stay away from home even on weekends, typically, it is a distraction from addressing the problem in the marriage.

4. Emotional Manipulation: The Guilt Games

There are three types of emotional manipulation.

a. **Manipulation by affection/guilt-tripping:** This strategy points to an imbalance in the power dynamic within the relationship, wherein the person who wants the relationship more will start to guilt-trip the other. Guilting can show up as overt pleading for attention or more subtly as emotional manipulation by doing something the other person wants and making it clear they now owe you. This form of give-and-take happens in relationships where one or both parties approach relationships as primarily transactional. They understand the give-and-take nature of things, and that would be the primary language of their relationship. Unfortunately, it is common in parent-child relationships where parents feel that because they have paid for the child's education and set them up for a good future, the child must now obey them in every big and small life decision.

I know a woman who suffocated a romantic interest with so much affection in the initial months that he was too guilty to leave, even when he knew it was the right thing to do. She would drive 30 km just to get a cup of coffee with him. She would wait three hours for a quick date with him. She would then visit him on holidays and impose herself on his free time in a way that he could not refuse because, well, 'she has done so much for me'. Even when he found a more suitable, compatible partner, he was too guilty to pursue it. Instead, he remained stuck with the manipulator.

b. **Manipulation by bad behaviour (passive-aggressive behaviour):** Manipulation with the opposite intent is also highly possible. I was once treated badly by a person who did not have the courage to say he wanted to leave. So, he acted awfully and disrespected me while waiting for me to make the difficult decision of leaving. This is not just a form of manipulation; it is abuse at its worst. Many relationships go through this kind of drama, wherein the other person is manipulated into doing what you want.

This is an emotional trap in which the partner is under the weight of obligation to agree to everything that the other wants. The trump card of this form of manipulation is often played when the partner decides to leave. When the manipulator enters panic mode and realises that the other person is likely to leave soon, she will start to make desperate appeals to have him stay by promising anything from changed behaviour to a great future. More than anything, she expresses shock that the partner wants to leave 'after all I have done for you'. If emotional manipulation has worked in the past, then partners reuse that trick with waterworks and pleas to elicit sympathy. Manipulating a person would not be required if the relationship were going well.

c. **Manipulation by threat of self-harm:** One of the vilest and scariest (for the receiver) types of manipulation is the threat that one will harm themselves if they do not get what they want from the partner. What makes this threat effective is the number of suicide cases reported in which a letter or message leaves a person's name as the abettor, who then faces legal investigation. The threat can be made in varying degrees. 'I am in pain because of you', 'I will do something to myself', 'I cannot live like this anymore', and the terrifying one of them all: 'I will kill myself. It is an almost assured way to get the partner's attention, if not exactly the reaction that one expects—sometimes that, too. The threat of self-harm leaves the person at the receiving end of such threats at a difficult crossroads. It is unwise to ignore such threats, even if they are empty. One also cannot submit to such manipulation. Either way, some intervention needs to happen. This is what the manipulator wants.

5. Anger: Death by Resentment

It starts as a minor irritation—watching them move in the same room, hearing their voice, paying attention to their questions, and even the very thought of them. Irritation is a sign of an unresolved major or minor issue. When irritation is left unaddressed for too long, it turns to anger. When anger is left unaddressed for too long, it turns to resentment.

One way many of us acknowledge a failing relationship is by a show of anger, which is another form of hurt. One can get aggressive and shift the blame for failure to the other person: Pick their faults, remember every time they made a mistake, and stack up substantial evidence. Folded into this is also aggressive name-calling, dominating body language, slamming doors, thumping fists, etc.

A show of anger is oftentimes dismissed as a person's inherent personality trait. Indian mothers, especially, choose to dismiss or minimise their badly behaved sons' ill-treatment of others as: 'He has anger issues, but he has a golden heart' or 'he is like that only, but he does not mean bad'. Even so, when one or both partners often express anger in a violent way in a relationship, it is a sure sign that something is not working in that relationship. Anger is a sign that we are deeply upset with ourselves, the situation, or the other person. Whichever it is, it indicates a broken relationship.

6. It's All My Fault: 'Blame Me' Blues

On this list, self-blame is perhaps the loudest agreement that there's a problem. At least one is clear what one is blaming the self for: The broken relationship. Yet it is a half-baked process in which we assume that the fault is ours entirely, and that we somehow should have been better in every way.

Self-blame jumps many steps in the process of understanding relationship breakdown. It jumps straight to the conclusion that 'I am at fault' by avoiding addressing the issue in its entirety.

The list of self-blame attacks is endless: I did not catch the signs early on; I got too busy at work; I did not earn enough money; I did not effectively communicate my needs; I was not available for the important events, and so on. This process often leads to lowered self-esteem and a dip in confidence levels, which may be challenging (but not impossible) to overcome. And yet, it circumvents the main issue: The health of the relationship that involves another person. Self-blame conveniently sidelines the presence of the other person.

7. Heightened Fear: Fight, Flight, or Freeze

This includes fear of loneliness, fear of failure, fear of what could unfold in the future, and the fear of starting over. When tightly gripped by fear, it becomes hard to see anything clearly. Everything seems foggy, and fear rules the mind, preventing logical thought or action. Fear is a big response to—and the cause of—relationships breaking down.

8. Self-Awareness: Mirror Moment

Folded into the process of self-blame is a more mature, self-rounded approach to acknowledging the status of a relationship. Stemming from self-awareness comes a process of taking accountability for our part in the relationship not working. In this reflection, we ask: What was my contribution to this dynamic? It is all too easy to jump into guilt from here, but a mature reflection would take accountability without shame.

9. Another Relationship: Rebound Rush

In the case of romantic relationships or even friendships, one sign of acknowledging the breakdown of the relationship is to quickly get into a rebound relationship through an affair or a casual fling with or without romantic involvement.

I know a woman who constantly changes her 'best friend' every couple of years. She goes out with the 'recent' best friend: Travels, parties, and does things together as friends would. And suddenly, one day, she would be seen spending time with another person in a similar manner, all but having neglected the now former best friend. Her friends found this behaviour strange, and they also noticed that this pattern repeated not just with friends but with her numerous romantic partners, whom she attracted and left for another soon enough. This behaviour points to the avoidance of a deeper problem. But it is a relational problem with the core issue being about how she relates to people.

Any of these signs indicates that a relationship is not working, and that we are using other means (rather than direct communication) to express the breakdown.

Repair or Release?

Now that you have acknowledged in your style that the relationship is not working, what are you going to do about it?

There are two main options: Attempt to repair it or consciously let it go. You may wonder about an enticing third option, too, which is to not do anything. You want to stay a little longer in the delulu bubble and enjoy its blissful perfection. But true acknowledgement of the problem means that you are consciously aware of it and willing to do something about it. Ignoring it while knowing there is a problem does not make it a genuine acknowledgement. By not doing anything, we are avoiding it or simply postponing the solution for another time in the future, hoping that, by then, it will simply go away on its own or resolve magically over time.

The Role of External Input

Most of us speak to at least a few people about our relationships—a friend, coworker, or therapist. Their feedback and responses to our sharing impact our minds and thoughts. Often, even when we don't seek advice, another person's impression of our situation influences us. These external sources colour our views and make us not only gain deeper insight into our relationship but also determine our decisions. This sphere of influence varies, of course. Those with a strong internal locus of control possess a louder inner voice and are more trusting of their own knowledge and instincts. They may listen to others but are less likely to let those views influence their actions much. The opposite is true for those who do not have a strong inner locus of control.

Using the advice of external voices is tricky because it can either cloud or clarify our knowing. Sometimes, we get stuck in a silo, an echo chamber, or a thought pattern that retains only the insights that are agreeable to our way of thinking while rejecting the ideas that challenge us.

There is a stark difference between helpful insight and noise. The external voice can offer both. The judgement of which voice to consider and receive and which ones to leave behind is entirely up to us. Our discernment decides how we use these 'helpful' voices. Ultimately, acknowledgement and action come from within us. So, while the external voice is necessary feedback, it is also limited in what it can do for us.

In subsequent chapters, I will take you through the various stages of handling a relationship breakdown, including the decision map of whether to repair the relationship or walk away. Meanwhile, when we look to Indian mythology for inspiration in managing relationships, there's one story that stands out about a character at a crossroads and what she did in a life-altering situation.

This is the story of Shakuntala and her lover Dushyanta.

Shakuntala lived her childhood in the quiet shelter of Kanva's ashram, where the days were marked by the soft rhythms of prayer, tending to the animals, and gathering fruits and flowers from the forest. She grew up learning to listen to the wind moving through the trees, to the wisdom of the sages, and the quietness within herself. It was in this stillness that Dushyanta found her.

He arrived one day, a king hunting in the wilderness, and their lives crossed like two streams meeting after a long journey apart. Their love unfolded quickly, as though it had always existed. Under the trees, surrounded by the silence of the forest, they spoke vows to each other in a Gandharva marriage (love marriage with the elements as prime witness). He left, promising to return for her. She stayed behind, holding his promise like a flame cupped in her hands.

But time passed, and there was no word of Dushyanta. Shakuntala waited, growing impatient and anxious, her longing turning into a fervent prayer. When she discovered she was carrying his child, hope and fear braided themselves tightly around her heart.

When she could not bear to passively wait, she left the forest and travelled to Dushyanta's palace. She saw him in court and stood before him with quiet dignity. But he did not remember her. A curse, they would later say, had erased certain memories.

In that moment, it did not matter why. He looked at her, and she was a stranger to him.

This was the decisive moment for Shakuntala. She had two choices: Beg and plead to force his acceptance of her or walk away. She chose the latter. She turned back towards the forest, not in anger but with her self-respect intact. She did not force herself to stay where she was not seen. She returned to the place where she was whole in herself, in the lap of nature in the forest. In time, the king's memory returned. He sought her out, and they were reunited. But that part of the story belongs to another telling.

What stays with me is Shakuntala's turning away. That was her moment of acknowledging fully that the relationship she had with Dushyanta and the love they shared in the forest were left behind in that moment. There was a quiet courage in her acknowledgement. In the space where love once bloomed and then was lost, she did not harden. She did not close herself. She carried her child and her dignity back to the world she had known before him. She belonged to herself.

We do not control the choices of another. We cannot force love to stay when it no longer remembers us (or wants us). But we can choose how we meet ourselves in those moments. Like Shakuntala, we can return to the place where we are already whole, even when a door we longed to enter stays closed. We can stand in the fullness of our own being and trust that we are enough. Whether love returns or not, we are already home.

There comes a time when holding on becomes heavier than letting go. When we stand at the threshold, we are often torn between memory and possibility, between hope and truth. And

Shakuntala was, too, standing before Dushyanta and facing the horror of his memory loss. But if we listen closely, a quieter knowing emerges. It tells us that release is not abandonment; it is an act of deep love for ourselves. To set something down is not to lose it, but to create space for something new to take root—within us, and perhaps, one day, around us.

Shakuntala realised that her turning away from Dushyanta at the palace was not an ending, but a turning. A soft exhale. A place where the story changes shape. This realisation may have come later during her still hours of reflection. But that moment of decision, where she chose to turn away with her dignity intact, was born from acknowledgement (not avoidance, anger, manipulation, or blame) that the relationship is not what she thought it would be.

An acknowledgement of the bend in the road makes the journey of relationship even more beautiful.

2

The Dangerous Promise of Potential: When We Wait for Them to Change

Many of us stay in relationships longer than we should, clinging to what could be instead of what is.

I have known Meera almost my entire life. We met when we were nine. She had this wild laugh that made you feel like the world wasn't such a serious place after all. We used to run around my neighbourhood until our legs gave out, make up elaborate stories about secret kingdoms and magic powers, and swear that we'd always be there for each other. We said things like, 'We'll be friends forever,' because when you're that young, you believe the saying of it is enough to make it true.

And for a long time, it felt like it was . . . until it wasn't.

As a child, I couldn't spot how flaky and unresponsive she was. It was all fun and games. Plans made and forgotten. Promises half-kept. Secrets shared, but never really held with care. I thought that was just how friendships were—messy, light, and playful. And when you're nine, ten, twelve, maybe it's enough.

However, as we grew up, something in me shifted. I started needing something more. Someone who could meet me in the depths of who I was becoming. I wanted to tell her about the things that scared me, the desires that lived quietly in my chest, the truths that felt too sharp to say aloud. But I couldn't. Not with Meera.

Whenever I tried, I felt her drift—a half-smile, a vague response, her eyes elsewhere. She was still that same girl, chasing something shiny, attention slipping through her fingers like sand. It took me years to understand that this wasn't just who she was back then; it was who she still was now.

And yet, I stayed. I stayed in that friendship longer than I should have, long after I'd realised I could not rely on her in times of need. I stayed because I kept hoping that *one day*, she'd get it. She'd show up. She'd become the friend I needed her to be. The friend she *could* be.

The thing about Meera was that she had a good heart. She was talented. She was kind when she was present. She had big dreams about who she wanted to be in the world. And I saw all of it. I *believed* in all of it. I was attached to that version of her—the one I thought would finally have that breakthrough, finally grow into herself, finally be the kind of friend I could trust with my messy, complicated heart.

Her actions never matched up with the picture I held of her in my mind. She was unreliable. She kept repeating old patterns. She didn't show up for me the way I showed up for her. And still, I waited. Giving chances. Making excuses. Investing energy because I was attached to the version of her I *believed* she could become.

But potential isn't a guarantee. It's a possibility. And possibilities aren't promises.

Among friends, this can look like:

- Sticking with someone who drains you emotionally because you believe *one day* they'll stop being self-centred or flaky.
- Being the 'therapist friend,' thinking if you're just patient enough, they'll finally *get it* and be the friend you need.

- Overlooking disrespect or lack of reciprocity because you're holding onto memories of when they *were* that amazing friend (or you think they *will* be again when life calms down for them).

That was me. All of it.

I kept replaying the good days in my mind, like old songs from childhood that still made me smile. Remember the time at that café when we laughed so hard, we cried? Remember when she surprised me on my birthday with cupcakes and candles? Remember when we talked about running away to the mountains and living in a little wooden cabin with a dog and no responsibilities?

I clung to those memories like they were signs of who she was deep down. But deep down isn't always where people live.

The hard truth? Sometimes we stay in friendships (and all types of relationships) because of the potential, not the reality. It's love for who they could be. And while that's hopeful and human, it can also trap you in an unbalanced dynamic.

By the time we crossed into our twenties, Meera and I were still friends, but only by name. We didn't really share our lives. She didn't really know who I was anymore. And I didn't really trust her with who I was becoming. It was too late to come into adulthood together and then change the friendship. Now we were just *there*. Two people with history but not much else.

I used to tell myself that maybe one day it would be different. Maybe if I waited long enough, she would finally be able to be the friend I knew she could be. But after all these years, I've realised something simple and painful: Waiting for someone to change doesn't make them change.

It only makes you wait.

THE MIRAGE OF CHANGE

We see countless relationships stuck in the 'waiting room' where the hope is that the other person will change and finally see us for who we are. The promise of potential is often too enticing to give up. It makes us hold on to the 'what could be', painting a rosy picture of non-reality or a probable future reality.

The belief in the person doing the waiting is that 'if this one thing changes', everything will be great. The success of the relationship is based on the conditionality of the other person's changed behaviour, or in them seeing things the same way you see things.

This sort of waiting occurs in all types of relationships: Parent-child, siblings, friends, co-workers, neighbours, and romantic interests. The most painful aspect of the wait is that we are often waiting for the other person to notice our value. We are waiting for them to tell us that we are worthy of love and are capable of having loving relationships. The pattern of waiting often starts in a parent-child relationship and, if undetected, continues into most adult relationships.

Many of us confuse love with the parent-child dynamic, where we hope that one day our parents will see us, love us, and accept us. This isn›t a conscious choice, but a pattern shaped by our earliest attachment experiences.

If you grew up feeling unseen, unloved, or like you had to earn attention by being 'good enough', you might find yourself drawn to partners who recreate that familiar dynamic. You over-give and then wait, hoping that this time—unlike your childhood—the love you long for will be given. It's not just about the person in front of you now; it's about an old wound crying out to be healed.

Psychologists call this an attachment style, and for many of us, an anxious attachment drives the need to keep trying in a relationship, even when it has long stopped working. I have discussed this in detail in the chapter on attachment styles.

In every case of waiting in relationships, the other person's behaviour is an unreliable variable, which can keep the person doing the waiting constantly on edge. The only reliable aspect is our actions and choices. The wait for the other person to see our value is a tricky mirage. Each time we approach the mirage of change, it vanishes, leading us further into exhaustion and self-doubt. The chase, therefore, continues till we get tired of our nonsense. The chase stops only when we understand that a relationship is not worth pursuing, and that stopping the pursuit is not failure on our part.

Many relationships stay hinged on potential rather than actuality, ruining what could be a better life for both parties involved had the pursuer only chosen to stick to reality as it is right now, and not be hopeful of a great tomorrow that may or may never be.

THE NOBLE WAIT: HOPE VS DENIAL

What makes it confusing for us to decide whether to wait for the other person or not is our difficulty in distinguishing the 'good' wait from the hopeless wait.

It's important to distinguish between hope and denial. Hope emerges from reality and the present moment—it acknowledges the truth of where things stand right now while remaining open to the possibility that things could get even better. Hope is rooted in reality, yet it yearns for a different, better reality. Denial, on the other hand, rejects the truth, clinging to an imagined future to avoid present pain. Denial sets aside the current situation as though, if we looked away long enough, it would cease to be true. Healthy hope empowers us to accept what is and still believe in our growth and healing. Denial keeps us stuck, waiting for someone or something to change so we can feel whole.

Waiting in hope for love and faith seems positive, but it is risky. You may be hoping for a good thing, but it is still about imagining a future that you hope will take a direction of your liking. Hoping for change in relationships due to fear, conditioning, or low self-worth is extremely harmful.

Many a time, even highly self-aware people can find this distinction between hope and denial difficult, leading to spending time waiting for the wrong reasons and the wrong person.

Glorifying the Wait

The wait for a relationship to ameliorate is often considered a noble value. But where did this ridiculous idea originate?

The classic story of a love that transforms is that of Parvati and Shiva. Parvati, the daughter of the mountain king, is deeply in love with Shiva, an ascetic. She undergoes severe penance and austerities for years. Her devotion melts Shiva's heart, who then accepts her as a wife.

Parvati's love and devotion are said to have changed Shiva's mind. Shiva, in this tale, had his own transformation, but real-life people may not have the capacity—or even the desire—to change.

It is not uncommon to find single women with traditional mindsets fasting and praying for the perfect partner. There are many stories of great faith moving mountains.

But this is a mythological story wherein Shiva and Parvati are divinely aligned. We mortals are not. In reality, without the inherent willingness of the party concerned, one's prayers alone can barely shift the situation.

In films and popular media, the idea of a love that is hard to get is seen as a challenge. We somehow want to prove that our love is enough to win them over. A 'no' is perceived as an invitation to try harder. The chase then begins. Eventually, the chaser is shown winning through sheer persistence, which may include stalking and even harassment, with intervals of waiting for the love interest to change her mind.

Indian regional cinema doesn't even mask such overt signs of chasing. These include tugging at her saree pallu and singing songs while running around trees as she makes horrified faces to get rid of the chaser. There are also manipulative acts of saving her from goons, tricking her into an isolated mountain top to talk to her, sending love letters and gifts via emissaries—the list is endless. In the end, she is seen smiling and accepting that the chaser is a true gem of a human. His crass behaviour and manipulation are conveniently sidestepped to show that persistence wins in love. One only has to wait for the other person to change her mind. It *will* happen.

There is also cognitive dissonance in the chaser's behaviour, wherein the chase gets heavier with time. The dissonance is in the belief that 'I have already invested so much time chasing this person, I have to now make this count, otherwise the time spent chasing goes to waste.' Here's where the stubbornness comes in, and it becomes a never-ending loop of chasing harder till you get what you want. Not getting what one wants after a hot and heavy chase—sometimes lasting years—often leads to a breakdown. The chaser is shattered and finds it hard to recover.

Early awareness of stopping the chase when things can be salvaged, or better still, to avoid the loop of the chase altogether, is the only way to protect one's self-respect.

Here's a beautifully apt story from our ancient texts to illustrate this.

A troubled man once went to King Vikramaditya's public court. The man was deeply heartbroken. He loved a woman who seemed perfect for him in every way—socially, economically, and in shared values. Yet, no matter how often he professed his love, she remained indifferent. He had tried everything to win her over, but she didn't agree. And he couldn't let go of the dream of a life together.

The wise king listened patiently and then called for his trusted minister, who narrated a simple story: A man once sailed a weak boat in a brewing storm. Confident in his skills, he kept rowing despite the worsening weather. Eventually, the storm grew fierce, the boat capsized, and the man drowned.

King Vikramaditya explained, 'Sometimes the wisest choice is to turn back while you still can. You are rowing a broken boat—her lack of interest—with only your determination to carry you forward. But love requires two willing hearts. If she hasn't seen your worth yet, she may never do so. Continuing will only hurt your tender heart.'

He added, 'Persistence is a virtue when the situation is right. But in dead ends, it becomes stubbornness that hurts us. Wisdom lies in knowing when to return to shore and seek peace for oneself.'

The man understood. With gratitude, he left the palace ready to release his pursuit and begin his healing.

Men and women approach the 'wait' differently. This could be due to social conditioning, but also the way the genders are wired for relationships. For women, the wait is often quieter and silent. It is even expected of her.

Traditionally, she is conditioned to believe that she is the emotionally stronger and more mature of the sexes. So, she must bear the bigger emotional burden of the relationship. If this means tolerating the partner's whims and idiosyncrasies, so be it. Many women also believe that it is okay to wait for a man to end his ongoing relationship so he can return to her. Wives feel that it is noble to wait for the husband to end the relationship with another woman and return to her. We are told, 'That's just how it is.'

Bearing the cost of the emotional burden is true for women in every type of relationship, whether it is a son, in-laws, or relatives. But this cannot be generalised. Men, too, are conditioned to wait silently. This shows up as the man's silent emotional suppression (being unable to share his true feelings), and the pressure to 'win' a woman's affection as though it were a conquest.

SCARCITY MINDSET VS ABUNDANCE MINDSET

'This is my only chance at love.'
'She is *the* best partner for me.'
'There is none other like him.'

These are all examples of the scarcity mindset that can lock us into the belief that 'it is now or never'. My own understanding that love can happen at any age came a few years ago when a friend's mother, aged 60, found love in an 80-year-old man, her Bridge partner at the local club.

The two fell in love and got married—her third and his second. The marriage did not last, but she has not let this failure dishearten her desire to heal from this heartbreak and open her heart again. This is an example of the abundance mindset: A belief that there are billions of people here, and many would easily fit into our idea of a good partner. It is up to us to continue the search with the belief that life doesn't end when relationships do. Her story reminded me that age is no barrier to love—and that possibilities exist far beyond our limiting beliefs.

The same applies to finding friends and companions who understand us and who can walk with us through the journey of life. Sometimes, friends fall off the path for several reasons. Hurtful as that may be, we don't have a choice but to keep moving on our individual chosen journeys. The faith that many people on this planet fit into our idea of a good friend is the first step in giving the friendship an opportunity to bloom. If it does, great. If it doesn't, it was an experience.

We don't wait for people to change for the better because it's noble or spiritual. We wait because we are afraid there's nothing better. This fear roots itself in the scarcity mindset—the belief that love is limited, opportunities are rare, and we are not enough on our own.

The path out of this fear is to gently cultivate an abundance mindset. Abundance doesn't mean pretending everything is perfect or forcing toxic positivity. It means opening to the truth that life is vast, and that there's more love, connection, and possibility available to us than we can imagine.

Simple daily practices can help us build this mindset. Gratitude reminds us of what is already good and whole in our lives. Openness invites us to receive new experiences and connections, even when they feel unfamiliar. Trusting ourselves—believing we can meet our own needs—frees us from waiting for others to fill the void.

When we live from abundance, we no longer wait for one person to change. We realise we are already worthy of love and connection right now.

The Cost of Holding On

There are emotional, mental, and even financial consequences to holding on to wrong-for-us relationships for too long.

1. Missing Out on Other Possibilities

The first cost to pay is the number of missed opportunities from holding on to the wrong person instead of discovering life and its many other experiences, including people. The more time spent on the wrong person means less time for exploration. But this does not mean one needs to repent the time spent hoping for something that did not turn out as expected. The cost of staying is paid from the moment one realises that it is not working but continues to stay for several reasons, such as fear of leaving or loneliness. The moment we realise it is not working is the best moment to leave. Staying on longer means we continue to pay the opportunity cost.

2. Emotions Drain from Unmet Expectation

Staying invested in a wrong-for-you relationship is a constant reminder that it is not working. Regardless of the route you take, you end up disappointed. This can be a huge drain on the emotions. Also, unresolved conflicts, both internal and external, lead to stress and burnout. All this in the long term leads to anxiety, loss of confidence, and overall sadness.

3. Loss of Self-Worth

The longer we stay in an unpleasant situation, the less we feel deserving of a better relationship. It is like the frog in the well that thinks that the well is its destiny. Unless you step out with confidence and allow life to show you new experiences, you will never know. You might start to believe you're not worthy of love, when the truth is, you've just been standing too long at the wrong door.

4. Constant Stress Leads to Physical Health Issues

Mental stress leads to headaches, stress-led migraines, and other physical ailments from suppressed emotions. Being in unhealthy environments for too long can normalise the stressful situation. However, the body retains and stores stress in the body, which can later manifest as illnesses.

5. Threat of Repeating Old Patterns

The fear of breaking up relationships that are not working can keep us stuck in old patterns. We stay stuck instead of focusing on moving to something better. Breaking out of patterns is a bold move. And no one but you can help yourself to make the leap out of an unhealthy pattern.

When to Let Go

There could be many reasons to leave a relationship—any type of relationship—that's not working. But certain obvious early signs are absolute no-goes to continue in the hope that things will change for the better. Here are ten red flags that indicate it is time to leave a relationship.

1. Toxicity

The most difficult part of dealing with a toxic relationship is the inconsistency at play. One day, they are nice to you, and the next day, they are not. It is difficult to predict when they might attack you in anger, using harsh words or make a show of sympathy and go out of their way to help you. This confusing flip-flop, when displayed by someone close, can be emotionally draining. Only awareness and the courage to acknowledge that this flip-flop is happening can make one see the truth behind the negativity, manipulation, and emotional harm. Often, these negativities outweigh the benefits from love, support, and respect. In such a relationship, there is also criticism, gaslighting, emotional or physical abuse, and an overall draining dynamic. Toxic relationships rarely improve and often get worse over time. The key ingredient to look for is inconsistency.

2. Lack of Respect

Any relationship, no matter the age difference, gender, class, or any other parameter, is based on mutual respect. Without respect, the relationship can only survive on transactions. If there is consistent disrespect, such as belittling, dismissing your feelings, or violating boundaries, it shows a lack of regard for your well-being. This is also hard to detect sometimes when, within the family dynamic, there is such rampant breaching of boundaries that some of us grow up normalising it. We begin to believe that it is fine to impose something on a close family member or loved one. It is rarely seen as a lack of respect till we find relationships crumbling all around us. Respect is fundamental to any healthy relationship. Without it, no relationship can survive the tests of time.

3. Repeated Lying and Betrayal

These are signs of a lack of seriousness in the relationship. It not only erodes trust but also creates an environment of despair where the liar cannot be depended on for anything at all, because who knows she might be lying about doing something and then not do it. Trust is the foundation of any healthy relationship. If someone repeatedly lies, cheats, or breaks promises, it indicates a deep-rooted issue that won't be fixed with hope alone.

4. Emotional Unavailability

This is also a difficult one to spot, as many glorify people who manage problems on their own without sharing with anyone else. This is deceptively seen as a sign of strength when it actually is a sign that the person is brushing issues under the carpet and not addressing them or giving them their due as they occur. If a person consistently avoids deep conversations, shuts down during conflicts, or refuses to acknowledge your emotional needs, it creates loneliness for the person at the receiving end of such emotional shutdown within the relationship.

5. One-Sided Effort

A successful relationship is a two-way street. If you are always the one making an effort, whether it is initiating conversations, planning meetings, or solving problems, it shows an imbalance that will leave you exhausted. This is also a sign that there are other priorities for the person, and she may not be ready for an honest relationship.

6. Control and Manipulation

This one is both easy and difficult to detect, depending on how loud and obvious the manipulation is. If the other person constantly tries to control your choices, isolates you from loved ones, or makes you feel guilty for asserting your needs, it is a major threat to the relationship. Healthy relationships have plenty of room for independence and personal growth. If these are taken away from you in a relationship, then it may be time to assess its health. A good test is to check in with your body when you are near that person (the body usually tenses and feels sore and on edge if it's an unhealthy dynamic).

7. Consistent Negativity and Drama

This is obvious to spot. If the relationship is filled with constant fights, misunderstandings, or extreme emotional highs and lows, it is emotionally exhausting for both parties and often not sustainable. The issues may be valid or not. The fact that there is no calm way in which to address them is the problem.

8. No Shared Values or Goals

If your core values, aspirations, or lifestyle choices clash significantly, staying together will lead to resentment or forced compromises. Think of big life decisions like wanting children, moving overseas, a place of retirement, money-spending habits, and core values like honesty and respect for others.

9. Feeling Drained Instead of Fulfilled

A good relationship should bring joy, support, and a sense of security. If you constantly feel drained, anxious, or unappreciated, it is a sign that the relationship is doing more harm than good. The body is a good indicator of how you feel around the other person. Do you feel soothed or tense?

10. Repeated Patterns of Hurt and Apology

If the relationship follows a cycle where the person hurts you, apologises, and then repeats the same behaviour, it is a sign they're unlikely to change. Words mean little without consistent action. A repetitive cycle means that neither the break nor the coming together is to be taken seriously. The cycle can repeat endlessly.

3

When to Stay and When to Leave: How Do We Know It's Over?

A friend's cousin, Rhea, was working at a fast-growing digital marketing start-up. The founder, a woman named Asha, was charismatic, confident, and always brimming with extensive ideas. She talked about revolutionising the industry, empowering women in tech, and building a culture where everyone thrives. At first, Rhea was thrilled to be there. It felt like an opportunity to gain experience, grow, and be part of something meaningful.

But it wasn't long before the cracks showed.

Asha carried herself as if she always had the final word on digital marketing, even when her strategies were outdated or ineffective. She dismissed expert opinions and made impulsive decisions that often undercut the team's hard work. Any challenge to her authority was met with coldness or public humiliation in team meetings. One day, Rhea was praised as an asset; the next, she was accused of not being 'dedicated enough' because she questioned an impossible deadline.

Asha's mood swings controlled the office atmosphere. If she was in a good mood, there were compliments and smiles. If not, everyone walked on eggshells. Despite her erratic leadership, Asha constantly spoke about building a family at work, of loyalty and grit. She promised promotions, stock options, and leadership opportunities 'down the line', as long as everyone stuck with her through the chaos.

For almost three years, Rhea stayed on. She told herself she didn't have a choice. Leaving the job felt like abandoning years of hard work, and she hoped things would get better. She rationalised that Asha was under stress, that all start-ups were chaotic, that if she could just prove herself a little more, Asha would finally recognise her true worth and offer her the stability and growth she deserved.

Her friends and family urged her to leave. 'You can do better,' they told her. 'You don't have to work in an environment that makes you feel so small.' Even former colleagues reached out and shared how free they felt after quitting.

But Rhea couldn't find it in herself to walk away. She fiercely held on to the promises Asha had made, to the potential she thought the company and Rhea's role had. She waited for things to change, for Asha to change. She stayed, even though, deep down, she knew better.

Sometimes, we stay in relationships—personal or professional—long after they've stopped being healthy for us. We think we don't have a choice, or we convince ourselves that we've invested too much to leave. We tell ourselves it will get better, even when all the signs point in the opposite direction.

In another story, a real estate agent in Bengaluru once shared with me about a client who had made a handsome profit by buying and selling property. When in his early twenties, he was caught in a terrible sibling war over ancestral property.

The way things were going, he realised that it was heading towards protracted legal battles. This meant that not only lakhs of rupees would be spent on lawyer and court fees, but he would also lose precious time running after something that anyway belonged to him. But his peace of mind and his family's well-being were far more valuable to him than the property, although it would have been a game changer for his financial status.

He decided to leave everything behind, not claim anything, and to continue with his life by creating wealth from scratch rather than lose his peace by interacting with his siblings and parents, who were spewing negativity at this time.

He invested in learning about real estate investments and gradually built a stable financial life for his family. He made a conscious choice to leave his family (kith and kin) behind and move forward in what was meaningful to him.

These are two different situations in which the real estate agent chose his peace of mind over an unfulfilling relationship with blood relatives. In the first situation, Rhea found it difficult to leave a job she had poured so much of herself into. It was a role she had once chosen excitedly, and sometimes choices can be wrong: We always have the right to choose a different reality for ourselves at any time, again, of our choosing. She couldn't find it in herself to choose differently, and that is a truth many people face.

The main question that the real estate agent and Rhea needed to ask was this: Is the situation likely to improve if I stay on?

In many cases, the answer to this is obvious. In the example of the real estate agent, it was abundantly clear that his family was not going to magically express love and compassion for him. Through their behaviour, they had revealed that their real motive was money. The agent noted, used it as information in his decision, and chose not to wait around to see what would happen.

In Rhea's case, Asha's controlling and dismissive behaviour was not going to shift overnight. Real change in such situations can only come from the person themselves—and only if they want it. Nobody can force a boss to be more self-aware or listen to feedback they don't wish to hear. When the desire is present, resources are plentiful.

We always have a choice in our relationships: To stay in a situation or leave it behind for something else. We get to decide how we want to be treated and whom we want to associate with. In the end, it comes down to whether—and how—we want to continue a relationship. Sometimes, we even explain away our actions by saying we had no choice at all.

The real question, then, is how do we know when to place our bets on a relationship—patiently continuing to work on it—and when to walk away?

Before getting into the indicators that suggest one might stay and keep working, or instead leave, let us first consider some key themes.

PAYING THE EMOTIONAL TAX

While a logical assessment of the pros and cons of staying or leaving is essential, we cannot forget that we are emotional beings primarily. Some of the things we want can be most irrational, making it impossible for us to find a logical reason for our decision.

The weight of emotion cannot be ignored. We can only understand and empathise with our emotions. We can rarely force ourselves to change how we feel. But logic is a different story.

Most arranged marriages in the centuries-old traditional Indian set-up, which has survived through the centuries, are just this. A logical assessment of the two partners based on height, weight, age, caste, class, education and, of course, a horoscope match. Arranged marriages of the old did not account for emotional compatibility, dismissing it often as a tax that gets taken care of when the basics are covered.

While traditional systems valued logical compatibility, they often overlooked the emotional toll this approach could take. This emotional tax is something many endure quietly, yet it accumulates over time. The emotional availability of the partner comes into play here, which makes the partnership (of any kind) a working relationship with an acknowledgement of the emotional investment from both sides. However, an emotionally unavailable partner—one who minimises or dismisses the other's feelings—creates a relationship wherein the partner pays a tax on the emotional burden that she or he endures. The tax can be in the form of time, energy, and patience—or all. When one individual does more of the heavy-lifting, the burden can get too tiresome to carry over the long term, leading to issues like burnout, depression, anxiety or more.

Accounting for the emotions is, therefore, important. Here are a few questions that help check if you are paying any emotional tax in a relationship.

- Can I express my feelings in their entirety without holding back? Will this person judge me for my feelings?
- Do I feel heard and seen in the relationship? Do they enquire after how I feel (not just physically)?
- When I express difficult emotions, do they listen to understand what I am going through? Or do they feel attacked?
- Are there no-go topics with this person when it comes to sharing how I feel?
- Do they make fun of how I feel? Are all my emotions (however big or small) welcome for expression in this relationship?

There may not be perfect answers to these questions, but if you spot an extreme response that causes you great degrees of discomfort, it often indicates that you are paying a heavy emotional tax to stay in a relationship with this person.

NATURE OF THE RELATIONSHIP

Some relationships are harder to leave than others. This is mostly due to our social conditioning about which relationships are 'for life' and which ones are accepted even with a shorter shelf-life. But our expectations from relationships and their longevity are changing. Consider the increasing divorce rates in the country today. Marriage was believed to be a 'rock-solid' relationship but is now on shaky ground. Although still painful, divorce is increasingly an acceptable 'out' of a situation that has stopped working. In contrast, blood relatives are believed to be for life, and difficult, almost impossible to let go of (you cannot replace your mom), while our chosen relationships, such as friendships and the people we take evening walks with or hang out with at the social club, are considered less permanent. These are only generalisations at best. Maintaining a relationship, regardless of the type, is a choice we make.

Writing of kin relationships, here's a story from the ancient Indian text of Vishnu Purana that carries a powerfully mature view of letting go.

King Uttanapada ruled Aryavarta, a prosperous kingdom in the lush northern plains of ancient India. Though a just and capable ruler, his personal life was a mess. He openly favoured his second wife, Suruchi, and their son, Uttama, over his first wife, Suniti, and her son, Dhruva.

Suruchi was ambitious and cunning. She used the king's partiality to her full advantage, determined that her son should be heir to the throne. Suniti, however, was different. True to her name, meaning 'good conduct', she was a woman of quiet dignity and grace. She didn't engage in petty rivalries with Suruchi, nor did she demand the king's attention. Instead, she poured her energy into raising Dhruva with patience, wisdom, and a deep devotion to Lord Vishnu.

One day, when Dhruva was only five years old, he approached his father's lap, hoping for affection. But Suruchi stopped him sharply. She told him that only her son had the right to sit on the king's lap and that if Dhruva wanted such a privilege, he would need to be born again, from her womb. The king, seated right there, said nothing. Neither did Suniti. Dhruva turned away, humiliated and heartbroken. In that moment, he realised a difficult truth—he might never receive his father's love.

This was a turning point. For a boy so young to have this clarity was remarkable. But Dhruva had been watching his mother all his life. He had seen how she carried herself with grace, how she chose inner strength over outward protest. Perhaps it was her example that gave him the courage to act with wisdom far beyond his years. Rather than fight for his father's approval or compete with Uttama for affection, Dhruva made an extraordinary decision. He chose to leave.

Dhruva turned to the one source of love and acceptance his mother had always spoken of—Lord Vishnu. She had told him that Vishnu responded to sincere devotion and would grant any wish if the prayer was pure. Dhruva decided to seek his place in the world, not through his father's love, but through divine grace.

Leaving behind the comforts of the palace and the safety of his home, Dhruva walked into the forest alone. There, he undertook severe penance. His practices were extreme, even for a grown man, let alone a five-year-old boy. He meditated for hours, chanting sacred mantras. He practised *Dharana*, single-pointed focus, the sixth limb of Ashtanga Yoga. He fasted, surviving on the bare minimum, and often on nothing at all—sometimes only air. He stood for days at a time in a single posture, unshaken, through scorching heat and cold.

Both the Vishnu and Bhagavata Puranas describe his fierce *tapasya* or penance. Dhruva gave up everything for his devotion. He withdrew his senses, mastered his body's needs, and surrendered completely to his faith.

After several months of this intense discipline, Lord Vishnu appeared before him. Vishnu, pleased by Dhruva's unwavering focus, asked him what he desired. Here was Dhruva's second defining moment. He did not ask for his rightful place in the palace. He did not ask for his father's affection or the throne. Instead, he asked for an eternal place—something no one could take away. He asked to be fixed in the heavens forever.

Lord Vishnu smiled and granted his wish. Dhruva was elevated to the skies as *Dhruva Tara*—the Pole Star. Unmoving and constant, the Pole Star has guided travellers and sailors home for centuries. It is a symbol of steadfastness and clarity. Dhruva, who once felt lost and unwanted, found his permanent place in the universe.

Dhruva's story holds a powerful message. In the closest relationships—even between parent and child—we sometimes do not receive the love we long for. And when that happens, we face a difficult choice: Do we stay and keep hoping, or do we leave and find a different path? Dhruva chose to leave. And though it was painful, it was also peaceful. His journey did not depend on anyone else's actions or feelings. It was his own path, rooted in his faith.

It takes immense courage to stop waiting for love from those who cannot give it. To walk away from blood ties is no small act. But Dhruva shows us that sometimes, choosing oneself and walking away is the path to peace . . . and greatness.

Persistence is a virtue in the right conditions. But there is wisdom in knowing when to return to ourselves. Dhruva didn't wait endlessly for his father to love him. Instead, he chose to sit somewhere no one could remove him from—at peace in himself and in his place in the cosmos.

There are two defining moments in this story. The first is Dhruva's realisation that he is not loved by his father in the way he would have liked. This is the most critical juncture of realisation because Dhruva had an important choice to make here. He could have continued to vie for his father's affections, and may have been even justified in doing so, considering that this is a parent-child relationship. In the vying, he could have played emotional games or competed with his rival for his father's affection, risen to the demands of such competition, and stayed in the 'game'. But Dhruva chose a more peaceful, albeit difficult path.

It was peaceful because his decision and what he sought did not involve anyone else but himself and his God. It was difficult because he chose the path of appeasing an unseen, divine force. This path almost entirely hinged on the power of his faith. It is no wonder then that the Dhruva Tara is a symbol of unquestioning faith in Hindu culture.

In the question of 'to stay or to leave', Dhruva chose to leave and find another path that did not depend on his father's affections or other people's minds and behaviour. This dilemma of whether to stay in a relationship or move on appears often in the relationships we choose. In a close bond—perhaps the closest—of parent and child, it is difficult to imagine there even being a choice in the matter. But this mythological story gives us an example of the availability of choice in all relationships.

THE REWARDS OF STAYING

The lure of what we stand to gain if we continue to work on the relationship is what keeps many of us in bad relationships for years, sometimes decades, even entire lifetimes. This is the ultimate trap—our belief that holding on will somehow magically make things work for the better. This holding on is often framed as the 'virtue of patience', but it can be a double-edged sword. It keeps people stuck in a traditional way of things, whether in marriage or in maintaining a bond with relatives. It is even more important, therefore, to assess the current status of the relationship, not its imagined future status based on fictional variables.

So, what are these imagined rewards we hold on to?

For many, it's the hope that things will get better, that love will return, or that the other person will finally see us and change. Sometimes it's the comfort of stability and routine, even if painful. Other times, it's the fear of regret: 'What if I leave and things get better later?' Or the weight of societal approval—remaining in a marriage or family bond because 'what will people say' if we walk away? We hold on to the image of what the relationship could be, rather than accepting what it is.

Take Tanvi, for example. Despite her husband's continued violence and emotional absence, she stayed. Why? She told herself that if she just waited longer, he might change. That leaving would make her a failure in the eyes of society. That staying was better for their child, even as the home environment remained unsafe. These hopes and fears kept her stuck in a reality that drained her emotionally.

It's a hard truth, but one that must be faced: Are you holding on to the hope of what could be, rather than accepting what *is*?

THE POWER OF INTUITION

Intuition is a quiet yet powerful inner guide. It draws from the subconscious—our memories, experiences, beliefs, and emotions—processing them without our conscious effort. A well-developed intuition often points us to the path that serves us best in a given moment.

Contrary to common belief, wanting something badly or knowing what you want isn't intuition. True intuition is a sense, an inner knowing, often felt in the body as much as the mind. It operates like a finely tuned instrument, giving you reliable signals—especially when you've taken time to understand its cues. Like a muscle, the more you exercise it, the stronger and clearer it becomes.

Here's how intuition can help in relationship decisions:

1. Sensing What's Not Being Said

You might notice things your partner doesn't verbalise, such as hidden truths, unspoken intentions, or simply that something feels off. Emotional intelligence sharpens this sense, but intuition often gets there first.

2. The Body Knows before the Mind

If your body feels tense, your stomach knots up, or you experience unease around someone, these physical signals often hold valuable information. Your body frequently detects subtle forms of dishonesty, manipulation, or hostility before your mind catches on.

3. Recognising Patterns Instantly

Intuition instantly connects present experiences with past patterns. You may suddenly 'just know' this is the same cycle playing out again, even before the facts line up. When you trust this instinct, you gain clarity much faster.

Learning to trust your intuition gives it a permanent seat at the decision-making table. The more you listen in, the more it speaks up.

Signs the Relationship Is Worth Staying (and Giving a Try)

Every relationship encounters challenges. However, those worth fighting for provide joy, respect, and opportunities for growth. If even one of the following signs rings true for you, it may be worth giving the relationship another try.

A word of caution: If there is any form of abuse, control, or disrespect, none of these signs can compensate. In such cases, it is wise and necessary to walk away.

1. You Can Be Authentic

In healthy relationships, both partners can portray their true selves—flaws, quirks, and all—without fear of judgement or rejection. If you feel safe to express who you really are and are met with acceptance, this is a powerful sign of a solid foundation.

2. There Is a Shared Vision for the Future

Even if the present has its challenges, having a shared sense of direction for the future is crucial. Couples in the same profession or an interconnected line of work find more in common as their intellectual compatibility will be naturally higher. If both of you envision similar life goals, whether that's career aspirations, living arrangements, or family plans, there is a reason to stay and continue working through the challenges.

3. Mutual Accountability and Responsibility

This is a basic requirement, and it can help two people tide over most issues. Both partners hold themselves accountable for their actions and emotions, and neither blames the other for everything that goes wrong. This type of shared responsibility can foster growth and maturity in a relationship.

4. The Relationship Feels Like a Partnership, not a Power Struggle

In a healthy relationship, both partners work together as equals, with complementary strengths and weaknesses. If you're not constantly vying for control or dominating the dynamic, it creates a sturdy foundation for cooperation and mutual support.

5. You Can Handle Conflict with Respect

The ability to listen without interrupting, disagree respectfully, and seek understanding, rather than just trying to win the argument, signals emotional maturity. It's important toevaluate whether both partners can navigate conflict resolution in a way that strengthens the relationship rather than weakening it.

6. You Trust Each Other's Intentions

Even when all your values don't align, if you fundamentally trust that your partner's intentions are good and that they have your well-being in mind, you can still build something good together. Trust in intentions is often the difference between minor issues and major betrayals.

7. Emotional Needs Are Being Met

This feels like a basic requirement. But even with fights and mistakes, if your emotional needs (affection, validation, understanding) are being met most of the time, it's a positive sign. It means that both partners are tuned into each other's emotional landscape and are actively trying to nurture the relationship, even if you may not see eye to eye on other things.

8. You Are Both Willing to Seek Help When Needed

A relationship worth staying in involves both partners acknowledging when things aren't working and being open to seeking help, whether it's through therapy, counselling, or talking things through. This shows commitment to improving the relationship rather than avoiding issues or letting them fester.

Signs It's Time to Leave the Relationship for Good

This is a difficult decision to arrive at. However, not making the decision only prolongs the problem; it does not get rid of it. These signs should guide you towards greater clarity in making decisions.

1. Your Core Values No Longer Align

Over time, you may realise that your core values, such as views on family, honesty, commitment, or future goals, are no longer aligned. If your fundamental beliefs clash in ways that cannot be reconciled, it may indicate that the relationship no longer serves either of you in the long run.

2. There's a Chronic Lack of Emotional Availability

One of the most painful things in a relationship is when emotional needs are consistently unmet (as in Dhruva's case).

If one partner is emotionally unavailable or unwilling to connect, it leads to feelings of isolation and disconnection. If this persists despite attempts to communicate, it may be time to move on. This is true for any relationship.

3. You Feel More Alone Together Than Apart

It's possible to feel lonely even in the presence of your partner or family member. This usually signifies a deep emotional disconnection. If being with your partner leaves you feeling more isolated than if you were alone, the relationship is likely no longer fulfilling.

4. You Are Living in Fear

If the relationship has become a source of constant anxiety, fear of confrontation, or fear of the partner's reactions, it can take a significant toll on mental and emotional well-being. Whether the fear is emotional, physical, or psychological, it's important to pay attention to these signs that things are not working.

5. Trust Has Been Repeatedly Broken

While broken trust can be rebuilt gradually, repeated breaches of trust—whether through infidelity, dishonesty, or secrecy—undermine the foundation of the relationship. If trust is continually broken and efforts to repair it are unsuccessful, staying in the relationship may cause more harm than good. Imagine living with the constant suspicion that you are being lied to. It is a huge emotional drain.

6. You No Longer Feel Safe to Express Your Needs

If expressing your emotional needs causes defensiveness, manipulation, or dismissal from your partner, you are not in a healthy relationship. A lack of emotional safety in communication can lead to a toxic dynamic where one partner's needs are never addressed.

7. You Are Making Excuses for Their Behaviour

If you find yourself constantly making excuses for your partner's hurtful behaviour or trying to rationalise their actions despite the damage they cause, it's an indication that the relationship is no longer serving your well-being. Defending them even when they don't show up for you means that you are not fulfilled. If you start to prioritise the relationship over your mental health, it is best to walk away.

8. You've Lost Respect for Each Other

This is a big one. Respect is a cornerstone of any healthy relationship. If there's a pattern of disrespect, such as insults, belittling, manipulation, or contempt, it undermines the relationship's foundation. If respect is no longer present and cannot be restored, staying may perpetuate harm.

9. You've Become a Shadow of Yourself

If the relationship has caused you to lose your sense of identity, self-worth, or passions, it may be time to leave. Some Indian wives are expected to lose themselves in a marriage in the name of tradition. In a healthy relationship, both partners feel encouraged to grow and thrive as individuals, not be consumed or overshadowed by the relationship.

These signs often reveal themselves quietly, beneath the surface. Sometimes, we normalise behaviours because they are familiar or because tradition tells us they are acceptable. But stepping back to assess the true nature of a relationship—beyond habit, fear, or hope—gives us the much-needed clarity.

Deciding whether to stay or leave isn't about predicting the future. It's about making the best decision with the information you have today.

Reflect on this: *What is the cost of staying, as I am, in this relationship for one more year?*

4

Assessing the Damage: How Bad Is It?

Aryan was 38 when he finally decided enough was enough. On the surface, things looked ordinary. He had a stable job in IT, a modest apartment he shared with a Golden Retriever named Kaju, and a few close friends who saw him for who he was. But his family was a different story—one that had shaped him in ways he was only just beginning to understand.

Aryan was the elder of two brothers. His younger brother, Rishi, had been diagnosed with borderline personality disorder in his twenties. Their mother, Parvati, swung between being the doting caregiver and the silent tyrant—her moods unpredictable, her love conditional. Their father, Ashok, had long ago disappeared into a fog of newspaper editorials and late-night news debates, quietly evading conflict by pretending it didn't exist.

For years, Aryan had tried to play the role of the bridge. The one who made sure Rishi didn't spiral out of control during family gatherings, the one who managed Parvati's exhausting, often impractical expectations, the one who called his father when the silences stretched too long. It was a balancing act that took a toll on his nervous system, though he had convinced himself otherwise. After all, this was his family. He owed them something. Didn't he?

The shift began subtly. It was during his weekly phone calls with Parvati that he first noticed the familiar heaviness in his chest before her name even flashed on his screen. She rarely asked how he was. The conversations were peppered with guilt-inducing statements: 'Rishi is struggling, Aryan. If only you were here more often.' Or 'You know I sacrificed everything for you boys. And now, this is how you repay me.' He would hang up feeling wrung out and strangely invisible.

The last straw was his father's birthday. Aryan had travelled back to his hometown, taking a day off work, planning a quiet dinner. It took all of 30 minutes before Rishi, triggered by a casual comment, exploded into a rage that culminated in broken plates and his mother weeping dramatically into her dupatta. His father disappeared to the veranda, staring into space. Aryan sat there, cleaning up the mess, offering apologies, and later driving Rishi to his therapist, as if it were just another Tuesday.

Driving back to his apartment that night, Aryan felt hollow. He realised that this was his role in the family—caretaker, scapegoat, peacekeeper—and it was a role that had consumed most of his adult life. He had spent so long managing the emotional needs of his family that he hadn't noticed his own life quietly slipping past him.

When he got home, he did something he hadn't done before. He sat at his dining table with a notebook and two pens. One black, one red. He drew a line down the centre of the page and titled it 'Cost vs Benefit'.

On the left, in black ink, he listed everything his family dynamic gave him:

- A sense of duty
- Familiarity

- Occasional moments of warmth
- The illusion of belonging

On the right, in red ink, he listed the costs:

- Chronic anxiety
- Guilt that never eased
- Sleepless nights after each call
- Physical exhaustion
- Feeling like a tool rather than a person

The right side of the page was longer. Stark. Honest. He then asked himself a question he hadn't dared ask before: *If these were colleagues or friends, would I still choose to have them in my life?* The answer was a quiet, resounding *no*.

But this wasn't a boardroom exercise. These were his parents, his brother. Was it even okay to walk away?

Aryan spent weeks exploring that question. He read books on family enmeshment, boundaries, and codependency. He journalled late into the night. He started therapy. His therapist introduced him to the concept of radical acceptance. His family might never change, but he could.

And thus he began assessing his boundaries with precision. He tracked his energy after every interaction. Did he feel drained? Angry? Relieved when it was over? His body was giving him data that his mind had long ignored. He noticed that he dreaded family calls for days in advance and felt hungover after seeing them in person.

Aryan made a list of non-negotiables. No more last-minute visits. No more phone calls that extended beyond twenty minutes. And eventually, no more calls at all unless he chose to make them. He wrote a letter—one he never sent—explaining his reasons. It was more for himself than for anyone else to read or agree with him. He needed to see the truth in black and white.

The decision wasn't impulsive. It was methodical and deliberate. He spoke to his therapist about his guilt. They worked on reframing it. 'Guilt does not equal wrongness,' she said. Sometimes guilt shows up when you do something new, even if it's the healthiest thing for you. Guilt often signals that you are breaking barriers, stepping beyond your social conditioning.

So, Aryan moved—not just emotionally but physically. He shifted to a different city, farther away, closer to his work and to friends who respected him. He changed his number, sharing the new one with only those he trusted. He deleted the family WhatsApp group that he had muted for months anyway.

It was eerily quiet at first. But then he could feel the expanded space. There was now space to breathe, to cook meals without rushing through them, to sleep deeply without waking in dread.

For years, Aryan had thought that disengaging from his family was a betrayal. Now he understood it was an act of self-preservation. A necessary boundary to protect his peace. He didn't need to justify it anymore.

Sometimes, healing is not about fixing the broken system. Sometimes, it's about stepping out of the system entirely.

WHY WE MUST ASSESS RELATIONSHIPS

Self-awareness and relationship assessment go hand in hand. One cannot happen without the other. The more self-aware we become, the better we're capable of assessing the health of our relationships—with others, and with ourselves. At the same time, the act of assessing our relationships reveals insights about who we are, what we value, and where we draw the line. It becomes a self-sustaining loop: Self-awareness leads to clearer assessments, and clear assessments deepen self-awareness.

In Aryan's case, his process of assessment was the turning point. For years, he had been running on autopilot in his family dynamics—fulfilling obligations, managing crises, smoothing things over, all without pausing to ask himself how it was affecting him. The moment he stopped to take stock of his feelings, something shifted. Sitting with his notebook, drawing up columns that listed the emotional costs and benefits of these ties, Aryan was able to see the truth that had long been obscured by duty and habit.

He realised that love or loyalty doesn't mean self-erasure. That he could care for someone and still protect himself. That his exhaustion was not just circumstantial—it was systemic, born from years of crossing his own limits to meet the expectations of people who rarely did the same for him.

This is what assessment offers us: Clarity. And sometimes (more often than we realise or admit) clarity demands courage. It may show us things we are not ready to see—the imbalances, the betrayals, the ways we have betrayed ourselves in the name of keeping the peace. But when we dare to look, we begin to understand what needs to be done.

I have seen people remain trapped in unhealthy dynamics not because they lack strength, but because they lack clarity. They go in circles, repeating patterns, wondering why nothing changes. A pause for self-reflection—a deliberate check-in to assess where we are and who we are to others—can serve as the spark that propels us forward.

Breaking patterns can take time. Assessing relationships, like Aryan did, can feel like opening a door you are not sure you want to walk through. But on the other side of that door is the freedom to choose differently. To choose peace. To choose yourself.

Early Detection of Problems

The most obvious and most important result of relationship assessment is the early detection of problems. A psychologist once told me that a single meeting with a person is enough to reveal several major character traits. More often than not, even those who pretend to be someone they're not get caught out if the assessment is sharp. Careful observation is all it takes.

We all put on shows of being goody-goody or the desirable baddie. But it is only a matter of time before the act drops. Seeing the real person without the mask is crucial for us to make decisions about how we would like to accommodate the relationship in our lives.

Early detection of problems helps with identifying niggling issues early on. We may be able to tell which minor issues are likely to balloon into deal-breakers tomorrow. Then, we already know what to look for. At the same time, we also know what to expect from the relationship, so we can decide whether that works for us or not. In most traditional arranged marriages, such assessment is non-existent, as there is no scope to explore compatibility at such deep levels. But even in marriages where partners have chosen each other, emotion and chemistry take on more of a role than the matching of values.

Misunderstandings and misalignments are often dismissed as lovers' tiffs and explained away with the idea that 'all relationships have issues' rather than encouraging a deeper assessment of the mismatch.

Preserving Emotional Health

Assessing the health of a relationship means that you are proactively investing in your emotional health. Imagine the long-term impact of dealing with an incompatible spouse, an incompatible boss at work, or even a parent. Not bringing to our awareness the health of each relationship can be detrimental to our well-being because we end up waiting until things turn for the worse before we take action. By then, we may already have dealt with numerous episodes of headaches, stress-induced illnesses, arguments, and fights, leading to even bigger issues like resentment and anxiety—the ultimate signs that basic issues have not been addressed.

We do not live in isolation. Most of our problems emerge from how we relate to others around us. In relating to others, are we also taking good care of ourselves? A self-assessment is a regular check-in process that ensures we are on track and aligned with our needs. Regular reflection on the emotional dynamics of a relationship ensures that both partners understand their emotional states and can work together to improve their well-being.

In the absence of honest assessment, if things are not going well, it could lead to emotional burnout and resentment. This often shows up in the form of feeling drained, frustrated and disconnected from the relationship. If things are going well, assessment can lead to an environment where you feel safe to communicate better. It fosters greater emotional trust.

Facilitates Communication

A friend who has an ideal relationship with his wife—a rarity today—says that the key to their relationship success is how much they talk. They talk about the smallest of things and the biggest of things. They can sit up all night talking and not get bored. There is room for each partner to express themselves without inhibition, as there is no judgement and an openness that every thought and every emotion is welcome between them.

Now, this is an ideal situation, and most relationships do not have this level of compatibility. But this couple has worked on this compatibility over the years. No matter what happens, they have at least a cup of tea together once a day. Given their hectic city lives, they find that the early morning quiet time before the rush of the day takes over, and before the children wake up, is the best time for them. They have created an environment of open dialogue where they encourage honest and compassionate communication.

Some of the relationship assessment happens during these conversations. But the start of this process was within each partner, where the individual took seriously the process of assessment and dared to be honest about what they needed within the relationship, and how they could contribute to the partnership.

Growth and Evolution

A relationship assessment is not just about looking for problems—it's also about recognising growth and evolution. It is necessary to evaluate what the relationship has taught each person and how they can grow within it. It may be that some relationships do not necessarily contribute to growth but provide support in other ways, such as emotional strength or being a good sounding board. These are valuable, too. But recognising the limits of a relationship, and what it can and cannot do for you, only comes with fair and honest assessment.

HOW TO ASSESS A RELATIONSHIP: METHODS THAT ENSURE BALANCE

I like to keep it simple. The assessment process itself need not be complicated. The difficulty, often, lies in how honest we are prepared to be with the assessment. If we lie to ourselves, then there's no point in the exercise at all. The simplest self-assessment exercise is to write the following on a sheet of paper, much like Aryan did:

- Three things that work in this relationship.
- Three things that make you feel hurt or unseen.
- Three things you need but are not receiving.

The answers will stare at you from the paper, and your honesty will shine through between the lines.

The following pointers greatly aid the process of relationship assessment:

1. Self-Reflection

Any assessment starts with self-reflection. This is a daily practice and not something to indulge in only when the going gets tough. It is a basic self-care requirement that helps maintain a healthy mental state. It is ideal if both partners have the habit of deep self-reflection, as the relationship stands to benefit from it. However, even if one person practises regular self-reflection, they will have a better understanding of the status of the relationship and the variables at play. It is essential to examine one's needs, behaviour, and emotional responses before assessing the relationship as a whole.

2. Open Dialogue and Honest Communication

A relationship cannot work if both parties are unwilling to come forward and talk it out. It helps to create guidelines for having honest, non-confrontational conversations. Yet there is no guarantee that these guidelines will be honoured when tempers flare and patience runs thin. For this reason, it is wise to set aside time to talk regularly about the state of the relationship. Within these conversations, you could introduce feedback loops where you give and receive feedback constructively.

Perhaps there is something small the other person does that annoys you greatly. It may seem trivial, but if you share it, the issue can often be easily resolved. For instance, I did not like a friend smoking in my car but hesitated to say so for fear of upsetting her. Once I found the courage to mention it, she simply stopped smoking inside my car.

3. External Tools

This is really important. Contrary to what many believe, these tools are not only to be used when everything has gone wrong, but especially when things appear to be going fairly well. That is when we have the mental and emotional bandwidth to understand matters better and to introduce simple yet effective ways to improve our lives and relationships. These assessment tools include journalling, relationship checklists, and, most effectively, relationship counselling. They can provide an outside perspective that we may not have considered.

External tools are generally most helpful when used in a professional setting with clear goals. Social media today carries a great deal of content from astrologers and energy workers who promise quick fixes—to get your lover back, to attract money, to separate two people, and so on. These are not valid external tools but purely entertainment. If such things truly worked, we would all be living in million-pound mansions and married to the perfect partner.

4. Balancing Expectations and Reality

This is part of the self-reflection exercise, where you check whether you are firmly rooted in reality or if certain unrealistic expectations are clouding your view of the relationship and what it means to you. Sometimes, we paint such a rosy picture of the relationship's role in our lives that we lose touch with reality and start living in a make-believe world, leading only to disappointment and grief.

At times, the person you are in a relationship with may also have unrealistic expectations of you. In such cases, you may need to intervene and bring those expectations to a more realistic level.

Relationship assessment should be done for all types of relationships: Friends, co-workers, bosses, romantic partners, spouses, parents, siblings—everyone. Regularly checking in on what the relationship can offer us, how much happiness it brings, and how much we must contribute to keep it alive are essential questions we need to answer.

Some assessments may make us realise that the relationship is not working, while others may point to certain aspects that we were taking for granted. An honest assessment lays bare our contribution to the relationship's health. Additionally, and more importantly, it helps us understand our choices and make them with eyes wide open.

SUGRIVA'S STORY: CHOOSING SELF-PRESERVATION OVER BLIND LOYALTY

In the Ramayana, Sugriva's life was torn between loyalty and survival. He and his brother Vali were once inseparable—

partners in ruling the *vanaras* and defending their kingdom. But things changed when Vali turned against Sugriva because he believed Sugriva had betrayed him, abandoned him in the cave, and stolen his throne. Banished from his home, stripped of his status, and living in constant fear for his life, Sugriva found himself in a painful dilemma.

Despite being wronged, Sugriva wrestled with guilt and grief. He still loved his brother. He still wished for reconciliation. For a long time, Sugriva lived in hiding, clinging to hope that things might return to the way they once were. But each passing day forced him to confront the truth: Vali's mistrust had turned to cruelty, and there was no safety or dignity left for him in that relationship.

It was then that Sugriva made the most difficult decision of his life. He assessed his bond with Vali—not through nostalgia or longing, but through clear-eyed honesty. He realised he could no longer be the younger brother who followed Vali blindly. He had to choose himself, his safety, and his future. When Rama arrived and offered his help, Sugriva saw a way forward—not one driven by vengeance, but by a desire to reclaim his life.

Sugriva's story is not one of easy choices. It is the story of someone who deeply loved his brother, but who came to understand that loyalty should never demand self-destruction. His decision to fight for his rightful place was also a decision to fight for his self-worth. In choosing to act, Sugriva honoured the bond they once shared while accepting that some relationships, no matter how deeply rooted, cannot be restored.

Many of us face similar crossroads in our own lives. We are torn between love and self-preservation, between what was and what is. Sugriva teaches us that the act of assessment can lead us to clarity—and sometimes, clarity leads us to choices we never imagined we would have to make. But when we choose ourselves, we choose life.

CONSEQUENCES OF NOT ASSESSING A RELATIONSHIP

Many of us continue to stay in bad relationships—or in relationships that are no longer adding value to our lives—because the process of assessing them demands brutal honesty. And if we don't like what we see, do we have the courage to take action? That is often the most painful part. So, we take the easier route: We accept these relationships, especially long-term ones, as part of our fate. We carry on without rocking the boat.

It is like stretching chewing gum until it snaps and makes a mess. We tell ourselves we will postpone the mess, hoping that things will somehow improve on their own. But postponing only delays the inevitable.

In Indian culture today, excessive assessment of relationships is often discouraged, especially if it goes against the collective ideal of maintaining social harmony. This is in sharp contrast to the individual-driven choices that are encouraged in the West. Yet our ancient stories tell us something different. In the Ramayana, Mahabharata, and Puranas, characters often take bold, even painful steps after deep self-assessment.

Neglecting relationship assessments—even in decades-old relationships—can have severe mental and emotional consequences. Here are just a few of the most common outcomes:

1. Build-Up of Resentment

When problems arise in relationships—as they inevitably do—we have a choice: Address them immediately or let them slide. Timely conversations, though uncomfortable, help maintain the health of the relationship. Sometimes they lead to parting ways, but at least the decision is made consciously and with clarity.

If we continue to avoid issues, resentment builds. Small grievances accumulate and snowball into major frustrations. Unspoken expectations, disappointments, and repeated hurts become too heavy to carry. One of the greatest dangers of neglecting assessment is the slow erosion of goodwill and connection.

I once had a friend who mocked my feelings. I explained how his jokes affected me, hoping he'd understand. But he laughed it off again. That was the last time I reached out to him. Sometimes, walking away is the healthiest choice.

2. Loss of Intimacy

A friend once told me about a man she was dating. Everything seemed fine until he began to open up about his life. But instead of sharing and listening, he would dominate conversations, speaking without pause and leaving no space for her thoughts or feelings. Despite raising this with him, his behaviour didn't change. Over time, she felt herself withdraw emotionally, unable to stay connected.

Intimacy fades when we don't feel seen or heard. When we take each other for granted or when we stop making the effort to connect, emotional and physical distance grows. Awareness of these early signs is crucial if we want to nurture connection.

3. Stagnation in Relationships

Relationships, like people, are meant to grow and evolve. None of us is the same person we were even six months ago. If we expect our partners, friends, or family to remain unchanged, we are clinging to an illusion.

Assessment is a way to acknowledge these changes—both in ourselves and others. We can ask: How have I grown? How have they changed? And are we still aligned in ways that matter? Without this reflection, relationships risk stagnating, unable to adapt to the new versions of ourselves.

4. Too Much Change

The other side of stagnation in relationships is when one person grows quickly, and the other is not equipped to manage the pace of that change. For example, if a wife once mentored her husband in growing part of his career, and over time he developed the necessary skills and rose to his full potential and independence, the wife might not recognise the sudden growth in him. She may feel resentful that he is no longer dependent on her for those things. Individuals grow at different paces, and relationships are healthy when they make room for such varied speeds of change.

5. Toxic Dynamics

Avoiding assessment out of fear can trap us in toxic cycles. The longer we ignore manipulation, gaslighting, or devaluing behaviour, the harder it becomes to confront. After years of tolerating dysfunction, we may even convince ourselves it is too late to speak up. But no amount of time justifies enduring harm.

Sugriva tolerated Vali's mistreatment for a long time, believing things might get better. But eventually, he saw that saving himself meant breaking the cycle. It takes immense courage to address toxicity, whether it has been weeks or years.

6. Inability to Reconcile

Without a clear assessment, reconciliation becomes difficult. We cannot fix what we do not understand. I have known people who avoid conflict to the point where they lose the ability to resolve issues altogether. One friend, an excellent team manager at work, avoided any personal conversations that demanded emotional honesty. She preferred relationships that didn't require intimacy or effort. But, over time, this avoidance left her isolated.

Conflict resolution requires clarity, courage, and compassion. And it begins with assessing what is working, what is not, and what we are willing to change.

Assessing relationships is not about finding reasons to leave—it is about finding the truth. Sometimes the truth leads us to a deeper connection and renewed commitment. Other times, it guides us to release what no longer serves our growth. Either way, clarity is the gift. When we assess with honesty and courage, we reclaim our power to make choices that honour who we are today, not who we were yesterday. And in doing so, we give ourselves—and others—the freedom to grow, evolve, and be met where we truly are.

Like Sugriva standing at the edge of his kingdom, we are always faced with a choice—to stay hidden in old patterns or to step forward into a life that fits the person we have become.

5

Leaning on Support: Friends, Family, and Professionals Can Help

Carl, my close friend, found himself at a difficult crossroads. At 33, living in a small town in Tanzania, he was deeply involved in his family's successful travel business, while also running a gym, a hotel, and an auto service company. To most people, he seemed to have it all together. But privately, Carl was struggling with a growing sense of unease.

His parents, loving but traditional, had begun urging him to marry. As their second son had come out as gay and moved overseas, Carl was seen as the one who would carry forward the family name and legacy. This unspoken pressure weighed heavily on him. He had dated several women over the years, especially during his frequent trips abroad, but back home, the dating pool was limited. Eventually, he began seeing Erin, a local schoolteacher.

'On paper, she's perfect,' he told me. Smart, well-respected, kind. Their families approved, and things progressed smoothly—at least on the surface.

But Carl couldn't shake the feeling that something was missing. Despite Erin's many admirable qualities, he struggled to feel a deeper sense of connection. They moved in, hoping that proximity and time would bridge the gap. For almost two years, Carl stayed, convincing himself that he should make it work. After all, he had already invested so much time and energy. His parents' hopes were pinned on this relationship. Erin's family was equally hopeful. Exiting now, he thought, would disappoint everyone.

Carl found himself growing anxious, restless, and often emotionally drained. Finally, in a moment of clarity, he reached out. First, to his closest friend—someone he trusted to listen without judgement. They spoke late into the night. His friend didn't offer answers but asked the questions Carl had been avoiding: *'Are you happy? Do you feel free to be yourself with her? What are you truly afraid of losing?'*

Encouraged by that conversation, Carl opened up to an older cousin. Over a long hike, they talked about family pressure, duty, and the weight of expectations. His cousin, having carved his own path, told him something that stayed with Carl: 'You don't owe anyone a version of yourself that isn't true.'

Finally, Carl decided to work with a therapist in Dar es Salaam. In those sessions, he began to unravel patterns he hadn't seen before—his tendency to suppress his own needs to avoid disappointing others, his fear of being perceived as selfish, and his deep longing for a partner who felt like home. The therapist didn't tell Carl what to do but helped him clarify what he already knew deep down.

Eventually, Carl made the difficult decision to end the relationship with Erin. It was painful, but also deeply freeing. His family was initially upset, but with time, they came to respect his choice. Carl realised that while he had to decide on his own, he didn't have to do it alone. The support of friends, family, and his therapist had helped him find the courage to act in alignment with his truth.

What Carl's experience shows us is that sometimes, when we are caught in the fog of indecision, it is the people around us—those who love us, who see us clearly—who can guide us back to ourselves. Whether it is a friend, a sibling, or a professional, the right support doesn't necessarily offer solutions. It offers a mirror, and sometimes a hand to hold as we find our own way forward.

YOU ARE NOT MEANT TO HEAL ALONE

Somewhere along the way, we picked up a story that healing is a lonely road. That we must walk it stoically, with clenched fists and a brave face. That strength lies in doing it all by ourselves. We carry this myth of the lone warrior who goes into the dark forest alone, battles their demons, and emerges scarred but victorious. And so, we isolate ourselves in our pain, thinking this is how it's supposed to be. That needing support is weakness. That sharing our story makes us a burden.

But healing was never meant to be a solitary process.

If you look to nature, you'll see that everything heals in community. A broken tree leans on the ones beside it to stay upright. An injured animal finds safety within its pack. Human beings, too, are wired for connection. We are born needing touch, presence, and care. We thrive in relationships. And when we are wounded—especially in matters of the heart—it is through the presence of others that we find our way back to ourselves.

We heal when someone listens without rushing us. When someone holds our hand through the night, saying nothing at all. When someone reminds us, simply by being there, that we are not alone in this. Compassionate witnesses are often the difference between staying stuck in our sorrow and finding the courage to move through it.

Healing requires safe spaces—places where you can take off the mask and set down your armour. Where you can be messy, uncertain, heartbroken. Not judged. Not fixed. Just seen. And in being seen, you start to believe that you are worthy again.

There is no shame in needing others to walk beside you. In fact, it's one of the most courageous things you can do: to ask for help, to receive love, to let someone hold space for your becoming. The lone warrior myth keeps you in survival. But real healing? It happens in belonging.

If you are reading this and thinking, *But I don't have anyone*, I want you to know—there is someone. Whether it's a friend, a therapist, a group of strangers who gather to heal together, or even a sacred text that speaks to you when no one else can. The right help exists. And you are not meant to do this alone.

Why We Struggle to Ask for Help

For many of us, asking for help feels harder than suffering in silence. We carry a deep-rooted belief that strength means handling everything on our own. It's in the air we breathe. Cultural conditioning tells us that the strong are self-reliant, that they don't complain or need anyone. Especially in times of heartbreak, there's a silent pressure to 'be brave' and 'move on' without leaning on others.

There's also the fear that if we ask for help, we will seem weak or dependent. Many of us have been taught that needing support makes us less capable, less in control. We worry that others will think we are broken beyond repair. And so, we put on a brave face, even when we're crumbling inside.

For some, past betrayals make the idea of asking for help feel dangerous. Maybe you reached out once and were met with judgement, dismissal, or betrayal. That kind of hurt makes it harder to trust again. You may wonder, *What if they let me down? What if I get hurt all over again?*

And then there's the quiet belief that no one can truly understand your pain. You might feel your story is too complex, heavy, or unique for anyone else to relate to. This belief isolates you further, convincing you that you have to carry it alone.

But these are all old stories. They are not the truth of who you are or what you deserve. The truth is, we are human. We are wired for connection. And some people can meet you with empathy and care when you're ready to ask.

When It's Harder to Ask for Help

Some heartbreaks come with an extra layer of silence—shame. One such category is those involved in extramarital affairs. These relationships exist in the shadows to begin with, and when they end, the grief is often swallowed in solitude. There is no open space to mourn, no societal permission to be heartbroken. The pain must be processed in private, with perhaps a trusted friend or two (if lucky). The emotional weight of such relationships—laden with guilt, secrecy, and disappointment—can be immense. Seeking therapy isn't just helpful; it's necessary. Untangling the knots of such heartbreak takes patience, self-compassion, and a willingness to confront the hidden grief.

In most such situations, men—compared to women—find it harder to ask for help. It is a combination of mental conditioning and the need to preserve their gender's image in a collective call for a show of outward 'strength.'

The advisers, healers, and mentors that everyone typically turns to for help may also find themselves in a tight spot when they need help. They may not have cultivated a support system for themselves. And, when in need, they simply may not know how to ask for help as they are not used to it.

Another situation where seeking help feels impossible is when dealing with a mentally ill family member—particularly when that illness is unacknowledged. In many Indian families, mental health remains a taboo subject, only addressed when it disrupts social functioning. A person's aggression, erratic mood swings, or extreme passivity is often dismissed as personality quirks. Family members are expected to endure outbursts, overlook injustices, and carry on as if it's business as usual.

But some conditions—like severe borderline personality disorder or narcissism—don't just affect the individual; they become a storm that everyone close to them must navigate. The family walks on eggshells, constantly adapting to unpredictable moods, gaslighting and manipulation, feeling the weight of responsibility without support. When the system itself refuses to acknowledge the issue, where does one turn?

Without family validation, seeking help feels futile. At best, one can vent to a therapist—but even that can feel like screaming into a void.

The Science of Being Witnessed

There is something profoundly healing about being truly seen and heard. Not fixed, not advised, not judged but witnessed with presence and compassion. When someone holds space for our grief or pain, without flinching or turning away, something in us softens. The burden we've been carrying alone begins to lighten, even if only a little.

Modern science now explains what ancient wisdom has always known: we are wired to heal in the presence of another. When we share our story and it is met with empathy, the brain releases oxytocin—the hormone of connection and safety. This softens the stress response, bringing a sense of calm to the nervous system. We feel safer, less alone. Slowly, the walls we built around our pain start to come down.

There's more. Neuroscience speaks of something called '*mirror neurons*', cells in the brain that allow us to feel what another person is feeling. When someone listens to us with genuine empathy, their nervous system mirrors our emotion. We sense an unspoken understanding. We felt. And in that moment of being understood, we begin to believe that healing is possible.

Validation is not about agreeing with everything we say. It is the simple yet powerful act of someone acknowledging, 'I see you. I hear you. What you feel makes sense.' This basic human need for recognition repairs emotional wounds at a deep level.

You are not weak because you long for such a witness. You are human. And healing happens faster when we are witnessed with compassion. It is not a sign of failure to need others on this path. It is how we are made.

The Power of Support

When Sita was abducted by Ravana and taken to the distant island of Lanka, Rama was shattered. He wandered through the forests, calling her name, his heart broken and his mind clouded by despair. The great prince of Ayodhya, the one who had stood fearlessly against demons and injustice, now found himself helpless. His purpose was unclear. His strength was buried beneath the weight of his sorrow.

Rama was not just grieving the loss of his beloved wife. He was consumed by guilt and self-reproach. How had he allowed this to happen? How could he protect the world if he could not protect Sita? In the Ramayana, this is one of the rare moments where we see Rama falter, not because of a lack of power, but because of emotional devastation. He is stranded—physically, emotionally, and spiritually.

It is at this moment that Hanuman enters the story. A *vanara*, born of the wind god Vayu, Hanuman was no ordinary being. His devotion to Rama was absolute, his heart filled with unwavering love and loyalty. But more than that, Hanuman possessed the gifts that Rama needed most at this time—clarity, courage, and a deep sense of purpose.

Hanuman becomes Rama's bridge from grief to action. It is he who joins Rama and Lakshmana with Sugriva, the monkey king, creating the alliance that will lead to the war against Ravana. It is Hanuman who offers not just his strength but his wisdom—encouraging Rama to stay focused on the mission of bringing Sita back.

And then comes Hanuman's greatest act of service. Alone, he leaps across the ocean to Lanka—his body expanding, his heart steady. It is there, in the gardens of Ashok Vatika, that he finds Sita at last. She is pale and thin, seated beneath a tree, surrounded by *rakshasis* who torment her. Yet, she remains steadfast, refusing Ravana's advances and threats alike. Hanuman approaches her with deep reverence, offering Rama's ring as proof of his loyalty and presence. He brings her hope when she has almost lost it. He promises that Rama is coming for her.

But Hanuman doesn't stop there. He allows himself to be captured so he can deliver Rama's message directly to Ravana. He sets Lanka ablaze with his burning tail, sending a message of defiance and power. He returns to Rama with the news of Sita's location and her unwavering faithfulness.

Without Hanuman, Rama's journey would have stalled in the forest of his sorrow. Without Hanuman, there would have been no way to find Sita, no path forward. Even a god, an avatar of Vishnu, needed help.

This is the truth we so often forget. No matter how strong we are, no matter how righteous, brave, or capable, we all need support. There will be moments when we cannot see the way forward, when our strength is not enough to lift us from despair. It is in these moments that the presence of someone who believes in us can reignite our will to act.

Hanuman reminds us that it is not weakness to need another. It is divine design. Even Rama, the hero of the Ramayana, found his strength again through the loyalty, courage, and compassion of his dearest devotee.

And perhaps, like Rama, we, too, are waiting for our Hanuman—a friend, a guide, a witness who will help us remember our purpose when we are lost.

Healing Happens in Relationships

No matter how much inner work we do on our own, true healing happens in relationships. The wounds that hurt us the most were often created in relationships—betrayal, abandonment, rejection, neglect. And so, it is in safe, nurturing relationships that these wounds can finally begin to heal.

When we experience consistent kindness, when someone listens without judgement, when our pain is met with empathy instead of dismissal, something shifts inside us. Our nervous system learns that not all connections are dangerous. We begin to trust again—not just others, but ourselves: our instincts, our emotions, our worth.

This is why healing spaces matter. Therapy offers a relationship where you can be fully witnessed and accepted. Friendships that are gentle and patient allow you to feel safe enough to be vulnerable again. Support groups remind you that you are not alone, that your story has echoes in others' lives.

Healing is relational. We cannot learn to feel safe inside ourselves without first feeling safe with someone else. Bit by bit, these new experiences create different memories in our body and mind. Slowly, they rewrite the old scripts that told us we were unworthy or unlovable.

This is how we heal—together.

Rohan was going through his second divorce. On the surface, he held himself together, showing up at work, managing conversations, pretending everything was fine. Inside, he was hollow. But he told himself he didn't need help. Therapy was for people who couldn't handle their own lives, and he was not one of them. His pride wouldn't let him walk into a room and admit he was lost.

Months passed. The loneliness grew heavier. Nights became longer. He found himself replaying old conversations, arguments, and regrets. Yet he stayed silent. Friends drifted away, unsure how to support someone who refused to let them in.

One day, sitting alone in his empty flat, he realised what his pride had cost him—not just his marriage, but his chance to heal. He was tired of carrying it all by himself.

Reaching out wasn't easy. Making the first appointment with a therapist felt like swallowing his ego. But slowly, as he spoke and was heard without judgement, something softened. His healing, long delayed by his isolation, finally began.

Sometimes strength isn't holding it all together. Sometimes it's knowing when you can't do it alone.

DON'T WAIT UNTIL YOU'RE DESPERATE

Too often, we wait until we've hit rock bottom before asking for help. We tell ourselves we can handle it, that things aren't *that* bad yet. We push through, hoping time will heal what's broken inside. But healing doesn't happen through endurance alone. By the time we're desperate, exhausted, or in crisis, reaching out becomes even harder.

Support is not just for emergencies. It's preventative. It softens the fall before we hit the ground. The sooner we open ourselves to help—whether it's a friend who listens, a therapist who guides, or a community that holds us—the less we have to suffer alone.

You don't have to wait until the pain is unbearable. You can ask for support before you feel like you're drowning. You're allowed to want relief now. Healing happens more gently when we don't postpone it until we are broken beyond recognition.

Asking early is not a sign of weakness. It is a sign of wisdom. You are not meant to heal alone, and you don't have to wait for desperation to prove it.

Where to Look for Help, Where to Find It

Carl's story reminds us we don't have to do it all alone. When life gets difficult, it's wise to lean on support. But it's essential to identify the *right* kind of support. Here are some places to look.

1. Friends

Friends are often our first go-to. The comfort of talking to someone who takes our side can be powerful. Sometimes, just having someone agree with us helps us process the situation, eventually allowing for a more balanced assessment. Good friends can also be bold enough to point out where we've gone wrong—and where we have been wronged. When it's the latter, they often get angry on our behalf.

Friends are accessible and, if they genuinely care, they'll make time for us. Different friends serve different purposes: we discuss work with some, social life with others, and relationships with a select few. Choosing the right person for the right situation matters.

That said, not all friends are dependable confidants. Some show up only for fun but disappear when we need deeper support. Knowing who's consistent and trustworthy helps us open up to the right people.

2. Family

Family can be tricky. Some siblings or cousins can be trustworthy confidants, while others may betray that trust. In my own experience, a few family members became my rock, while others judged me harshly after I shared vulnerable truths.

'Why don't you just heal and move on?' is easier said than done. Some family members can balance emotional support with objectivity. Others can't. But I've often been surprised by unexpected sources of support—those whose actions matched their words.

It's important to know who can genuinely be there for you. When you open up, choose wisely.

3. Therapists and Counsellors

Therapy is often a reliable route. While friends and family may offer time and advice, they aren't trained to guide us objectively. They might not have the insight or experience to fully understand our situation.

Professionals are trained to see the bigger picture and identify archetypes. They don't have a vested interest in the outcome; their primary concern is your well-being. A good therapist looks beyond surface details, delving into your background and patterns to offer guidance that's not just comforting but constructive. They provide deeper emotional and psychological clarity—something even the most well-meaning friends can't always give.

4. Support Groups and Communities

Support groups—in-person or online—offer validation through shared experiences. It is amazing how many people would have gone through experiences similar to ours. They remind us that we're not alone. Hearing how others coped can provide ideas for strategies, though their advice may be one-sided. These groups are best used for emotional validation and general coping mechanisms, not as sources for decisive action. Use them as supportive spaces, but cautiously because such spaces can often turn into bashing grounds with lost objectivity.

5. Spiritual or Religious Advisors

When other avenues feel closed, many turn to spiritual or religious guidance. Marriage counselling in churches, astrological counselling in temples, tarot, or psychic readings—all are common. Social media is full of mystical 'quick fixes', though their reliability varies. Numerous fake Gurus are ready to prey on people's vulnerabilities. Setting clear boundaries on the type and extent of guidance—and carrying our common sense with us—usually helps avoid being conned. The real challenge, though, is that discernment is the hardest to summon when vulnerability mixes with the desperation for quick solutions.

That said, a trusted spiritual guide can offer wisdom and moral grounding, especially when their intention is genuine care. Spiritual advice often touches on karma and destiny, offering a larger perspective that can bring comfort during challenging times. But remember—no one can predict your life path with certainty.

6. Books, Podcasts, and Expert Resources

Books and podcasts are excellent for self-education. For example, a friend once dated someone with a genius IQ and felt unprepared. She read books about the challenges and expectations of such relationships and found helpful insights.

This kind of learning is like snacking on information—bite-sized, useful, and empowering. It's not personal advice, but it expands understanding and equips us with knowledge for specific situations.

How to Recognise the Right Help

This is perhaps the hardest part. How do we know if the advice we are getting is truly helpful? The short answer is: It isn't easy. If it triggers an 'aha' moment—'Why didn't I think of that before?'—then it is probably helpful. Often, we have to filter advice carefully.

Here are a few things to keep in mind when evaluating external guidance:

1. Objectivity and Non-Judgement

Helpful guidance is balanced, not biased. It gently leads us to a clearer understanding rather than pushing a specific outcome.

For instance, I once confided in a friend about a conflict at work. Over time, she became so aligned with my story that she stopped being objective—she just wanted me to 'win'. It felt good at first, but it wasn't useful. Later, a neutral third party gave me the clarity I needed. True support isn't just about validation—it's about honest perspective.

2. Empowerment vs Dependency

Be cautious with advisers who create dependency. Some spiritual gurus, energy healers, or even therapists can encourage you to rely on them for every decision. In times of uncertainty, we might welcome this, but it weakens our ability to make decisions.

Healthy guidance empowers you to make your own choices. If you notice yourself unable to decide without consulting someone, it's time to re-evaluate the dynamic.

3. Alignment with Core Values

Ask if the advice resonates with your core values. A non-believer being told to perform rituals will find little value in that suggestion. Similarly, a member of the LGBTQ+ community seeking guidance from someone who can't understand their experience may not receive relevant help.

The advice you follow should feel authentic and aligned with who you are.

4. Experience and Expertise

Life experience matters. Someone who has weathered various life challenges often offers nuanced advice. But be cautious—advanced age doesn't automatically mean life experience. Also, life experience alone doesn't guarantee wisdom or balance.

When possible, seek professionals or mentors who combine personal insight with relationship expertise. Look for practical, actionable guidance rather than theoretical ideas.

5. Practical and Actionable Guidance

Talking endlessly about the problem won't move us forward. A good adviser helps us chart a path out of the situation.

For example, when my friend heard about my work problem and gave me a few neutral insights, my sharing felt meaningful as it gave me a new perspective. It helped me change my approach to the problem. While we may not have great advisers around us all the time, a fresh perspective can change everything.

Ask whether the advice includes concrete steps. Abstract support is valuable, but action leads to change.

Where Not to Seek Help

Knowing where *not* to turn is just as important as knowing where to look.

1. Gossip and Social Media

Avoid friends who gossip. They are unlikely to respect your privacy, and becoming part of their gossip chain risks your reputation.

Similarly, avoid cryptic or emotional social media posts about personal struggles. They invite unqualified opinions and increase vulnerability without offering real support.

2. People with a History of Toxic Relationships

This isn't about judgement but about protection. People stuck in cycles of difficult relationships may, often without realising it, project their unresolved pain onto others. Their advice may be skewed by personal trauma.

3. One-Sided Opinions

Be cautious of extreme perspectives. People who've endured bitter divorces or hold overly idealistic views may, understandably, find it hard to offer balanced advice. Their experiences can cloud their ability to be neutral.

4. Unqualified Self-Help Gurus

Many self-proclaimed gurus and influencers lack the necessary training or expertise to guide others. They often rely on flashy marketing rather than real knowledge. Research their credibility before following their advice.

5. Advice That Pressures You

True support offers space, not coercion. If an adviser pressures you to take a certain path, they are likely emotionally invested in the outcome or manipulating you. Advice should help you see different possibilities—not dictate what you must do.

How to Identify Help That Isn't in Your Favour

Sometimes it's hard to spot when help isn't helpful. Here's what to watch for:

1. Hidden Agenda

If someone offers unsolicited advice, consider whether they have an agenda. Parents pushing reconciliation in a broken marriage, or single friends encouraging a break-up, may be acting from self-interest. Always question who benefits from the advice.

2. Emotional Manipulation

Some ego-led helpers may guilt-trip you or try to control your decisions, often based on their own fears or regrets. They may mean well but strip away your agency in the process.

3. Lack of Nuanced Understanding

Relationship dynamics are rarely simple. Good advice considers multiple perspectives. Beware of guidance that dismisses complexity and offers black-and-white solutions.

4. Encouraging Inaction or Harmful Action

Advice that keeps you stuck—or escalates conflict—is dangerous. Neither urging passive endurance nor pushing aggressive retaliation is helpful if it doesn't align with your needs.

The relationship, and the decisions, are ultimately yours.

5. A Pattern of Bad Advice

If someone has repeatedly given you poor advice, it's a red flag. Learn from past experience. If their input hasn't served you before, it's unlikely to do so in the future.

Choosing the right support is both an art and a practice in discernment. Seek help that empowers, respects your agency, and guides you towards clarity, not confusion. Healing doesn't happen in isolation, but neither should it happen at the cost of your inner wisdom.

6

Identifying the Healing Path: The Modalities and Approaches at Your Disposal

A few months ago, I was sitting at a nail salon in my neighbourhood, lazily scrolling through my phone while waiting for my turn. The faint whirr of hair dryers and the quiet clinking of tools against glass bowls created a soothing background hum, but my attention was drawn to a young woman seated a few chairs away. She was getting her nails painted a deep red, speaking casually on speakerphone with a male friend. It wasn't hard to overhear.

Through their conversation, I gathered something surprising. She was getting married the next day. Her friend on the line was clearly caught off guard. 'Wait . . . you're getting married? To your boyfriend?' he asked, incredulous.

'No,' she replied flatly, eyes steady on her manicure. 'He's getting married tomorrow because his family forced him. So, I'm getting married, too. On the same day.'

'To whom?' her friend asked after a long silence.

'It's arranged,' she said. 'The only condition I had was that he should marry me tomorrow.'

She wasn't angry. She wasn't crying. She was determined. Her face betrayed no emotion, her voice calm. It was as if she had already shut the door on the past and was now simply going through the motions of what came next.

As I sat there watching her, I wondered: Is this a good idea? Is this revenge after heartbreak, or something else entirely? Maybe it was a way for her to reclaim control. Or maybe it was a costly rivalry, one with many lives at stake—hers, her new husband's, and the man to whom she was still somehow tethered. Was this revenge worth it? And if it was, did it taste sweet?

THE ROLE OF REVENGE IN HEALING

When a relationship breaks due to betrayal, humiliation, being replaced too soon, or not getting the closure one deserves, the urge for revenge often runs high. Especially when pride is wounded, our sense of dignity and self can slip quietly into the background. Even the most rational among us may find ourselves fantasising about retribution. The human mind is complex, and we can seek to avenge being wronged in a range of ways—from badmouthing the ex to mutual friends, to stalking their social media and rejoicing in their failures, to the extremes of wanting to destroy what they love most. And everything in between.

But is revenge ever truly satisfying? Maybe for a moment, it can offer a fleeting sense of triumph. Yet the process of taking revenge comes with a heavy price: It prolongs our attachment to the person we need to be moving away from. Instead of creating distance, we remain emotionally entangled, feeding the very bond we are desperate to sever.

Revenge is a double-edged sword. It can keep us stuck in the story we are trying to leave behind. Sometimes, the damage we cause—to them or ourselves—is too severe to justify the act. And in some cases, we end up harming ourselves in a desperate bid to project an image to someone who has long since moved on.

Indifference Is the Sweetest Revenge

A couple of years ago, a viral video on social media left me quite shaken. It depicted a woman in her late twenties desperately trying to break open the iron gates and step inside a wedding venue where her boyfriend was getting married.

The woman screamed, banged on the gates, and attempted to climb over them to no avail. Later reports circulating on the viral video thread revealed that the boy had moved on without ending their relationship. When she discovered that very morning that he was marrying another woman, she made a frantic bid to talk to him, to understand what had happened and what she had done so wrong. She was beside herself, in deep shock and desperation, unwilling to lose perhaps the only relationship in which she had placed all her faith.

According to reports, passers-by pacified the woman, and when she fainted, she was taken to a nearby medical centre. No further news emerged about her journey after this incident. However, I often think about her and wonder what her path to recovery entailed.

In both these cases, the women put their former partners up on pedestals that they didn't deserve. Marrying a stranger on the same day so as not to be left behind, or creating a scene outside the wedding venue, are not acts of revenge. They are desperate cries for help to heal and to come back home to oneself. The women did what they thought was best at the time. They had to express their anger and hurt in some form, and they found the method that was best available to them with the resources at their disposal. Healing would come to them slowly, at a quiet time when they sat by themselves and thought things through.

Those healing from heartbreak have every right to feel the full range of emotions that surface. Often, the pain is not just from one disappointment but from the echo of many unhealed heartbreaks of the past. Healing is, at its core, a private process, though support from community and guides can help. When thoughts of revenge arise, it can be powerful to wear a stoic exterior. We owe no one—least of all those who hurt us—the raw truth of our inner turmoil.

In most such cases, when moving away from a relationship that is broken, indifference is a safe behaviour to rely on. Being stoic, neither friendly nor rude, neither angry nor in grief, neither ecstatic nor disappointed but a poker face of indifference, is the safest bet when one doesn't know how to behave in such awkward situations. Indifference is the best revenge because it immediately tells the other person that their importance was because of us. They were special because we made them so. We take back our power in a way that is graceful and dignified. No drama or fuss. Plain indifference. Even better is to outgrow people. *That* is real success.

There is a thin line between justice and bitterness. We feel that we are meting out justice by righting the wrong inflicted on us. But who is to say what is justified? When we are sitting in a cloud of hurt pride, we cannot look ahead clearly. And that realisation should be reason enough to hold back and not do anything we would later regret.

A wealthy businessman, hurt by a girlfriend who wanted to part ways, made a list of every small item he had bought for her, including gifts given over the years. He sent her the total on a detailed sheet. The girl laughed at the list and was now even more certain of her decision to leave. The man was being transactional in the relationship, and even in the break-up. She returned every last paisa and was glad to be rid of such transactions.

What happens when revenge fuels growth after a relationship break-up? And this can be any type of relationship—even sibling rivalry or friendships gone sour. What if the revenge story has an unlikely but desirable successful outcome? Many dive into work, for example, while going through a break-up or relationship stress. Their goal is to gun for success—and it may even work—but, in the end, even this is only a distraction from healing. It takes us away from the centre of our being and diverts us by giving us another goal. In some cases, therapists may recommend distraction—but only for a limited time and in specific situations, not when it postpones or circumvents the healing process.

Success achieved through anger directed at work is often an adrenaline-fuelled burst of passion, difficult to sustain over prolonged periods of time or even replicate. Revenge leading to growth is also temporary and a matter of chance. We stand to hurt ourselves more than we already are by setting unrealistic expectations of what we should achieve and what our recovery should look like after a relationship gone bad. Trying to force one area of life to compensate for another almost surely sets us up for disappointment.

Revenge is a great motivator for major love-, lust-, or obsession-based crimes of passion. It can derail the strongest logic and make the avenger pursue his prey with single-minded focus.

When we face heartbreak, we usually have only three options: Seek revenge, stay stuck, or heal. The first, as we know, offers the illusion of karmic justice, and that we have enforced it. So, we may feel powerful for the moment, but we remain entangled in the story instead of freeing ourselves. This delays the ending of that relationship cycle. It could even take lifetimes to end.

Staying stuck is also a choice we make. Our story does not progress unless we take the next step. Healing, then, becomes the only real option. To move forward from any relationship, we *have* to heal. The question is: How?

Why Healing Is Difficult

Healing from heartbreak—whether romantic, familial, or personal—is not just about time; it's about actively confronting pain. Several psychological, emotional, and cultural factors make it challenging:

1. The Attachment Trap

Humans are wired for connection and detaching from someone we loved feels unnatural. It stresses both body and mind. It takes plenty of effort to let that attachment go, even as we wonder what we will do with the empty space left behind.

2. Identity Loss

Relationships shape our identity. When they break, we question who we are without them. This is especially true for socially sanctioned relationships that come under severe scrutiny from family, friends, and neighbours.

3. The Ego Factor

Heartbreak wounds our ego as much as our emotions. The pain of rejection or betrayal often feels personal, even when it's not. Most healing work requires restoring our confidence, self-respect, and mental balance in the absence of that relationship. The work is mostly internal and solitary, as it involves our ego. And external help can only go so far.

4. Healing Requires Facing the Pain

Many avoid healing because it requires confronting emotions they'd rather suppress. It can be extremely painful, and in cases where we find it hard to manage alone, it is best to seek professional help and have a therapist guide us through the tougher parts.

5. The Fear of Letting Go

Moving on often feels like losing a part of ourselves. There's a deep-rooted fear that letting go invalidates the past. It also means sitting with uncertainty—facing a void with nothing yet to replace what was lost.

Healing isn't just about forgetting; it's about learning, integrating, and finding a new way forward without losing oneself. It is a slow and tiring process, but with the right mindset and determination, it can allow us to know ourselves better and grow into stronger, wiser human beings.

Importance of Healing Now Rather than Later

That we will have to heal at some point is a given. But what happens if we don't work on our healing promptly?

1. Unhealed Wounds Manifest Elsewhere

Think of the boss who fought with her husband at home in the morning and reached the office in a huff, only to yell at the door attendant. The door attendant yells at the peon, and the peon returns home and yells at his wife, who has nothing to do with the boss's domestic issues. The smallest of disagreements can lead to such a chain of undesirable events. A deep emotional wound can do far more damage than may be visible. It affects mental health, relationships, and even physical well-being.

2. Healing Restores Power

In relationships, there is a sharing of energy that distributes power among the givers in the equation. One person leaving or changing the dynamic leaves the energy scattered. It is essential to take our energy back. This is easier said than done, especially if you were trusting and giving in the relationship. But taking your energy back is vital to moving on and reclaiming control over your life.

3. Time Alone Doesn't Heal; Intentional Effort Does

The age-old adage that time heals everything is nice to hear in the moment, but along with time, we also need to show intent and act towards our healing. Active healing is required to prevent resentment from festering, which is sure to happen if things are left unresolved in our minds and hearts.

4. The Spiritual Aspect of Healing

In many traditions, healing isn't just emotional—it's about alignment with dharma and purpose. It is like leaving a door open even when you know that you are not going to go down that path anymore. The open door leads to constant tension and stress about what or who could re-enter through it. It is a subconscious anxiety that can rob you of precious energy. Not closing business properly, such as leaving legal paperwork undone even years after separation and a split relationship, can be draining.

Healing isn't only about feeling better; it is also about becoming whole and reclaiming your life. Healing can start almost immediately after heartbreak if you are open and accepting of the process. Some of us prefer to distract ourselves and jump into life's next excitement without fully addressing the damage caused by the derailment of the current relationship, or its completion, whichever the case. In such situations, healing happens at a later date—rather forcefully, through an illness or an untimely epiphany—where you have to drop everything and sit with your body and mind as you heal from past traumas.

The big question is: How to heal? Which is the best path to take? Indian mythology is full of stories modelling characters who chose various pathways to heal from unpleasant life experiences, shocks, and setbacks. Broadly, however, there are two routes we can take—going inward and looking outward—with two primary types of healing under each. Within these four types of modalities fall most of the healing work we do.

Going Inward

Introspective Healing

This type of going inward is aimed at healing through self-discovery, wisdom, and transformation through deep knowledge, penance, and meditation. Jnana or knowledge involves understanding the self: My needs at this time; how I understand things; my role, if any, in the events that transpired; and the big picture. The second part of this, Tapasya, is faith-based and involves trusting that the universe's healing energy will do its job if we call upon her and trust her with the mind and body.

Gargi Vachaknavi is a historical figure mentioned in the Brihadaranyaka Upanishad. Gargi was born into a learned family in Vedic India, a time when only a few women were able to engage in deep intellectual and spiritual pursuits. From an early age, she showed a sharp mind, absorbing the teachings of the Vedas with unmatched brilliance. However, due to a personal loss—one where she either lost a loved one or was denied marriage due to her scholarly ambitions—she was left shattered.

Rather than allowing societal rejection or heartbreak to consume her, Gargi withdrew from conventional life and immersed herself in the path of Jnana (knowledge). She became a lifelong seeker of truth, focusing on *Brahmavidya*—the ultimate knowledge of existence. Unlike those who found solace in companionship, Gargi sought clarity in philosophy.

Her wisdom became legendary, leading her to the court of King Janaka, where she famously challenged the revered sage Yajnavalkya, questioning him about the nature of the universe, consciousness, and the eternal soul. Her deep understanding stunned the assembly, proving that intellectual and spiritual growth can be a path to healing.

Gargi's story proves that some wounds require emotional closure—some are healed by expanding the mind, seeking higher truths, and finding purpose beyond personal pain. Instead of letting heartbreak define her, she became one of the greatest philosophers of her time, proving that wisdom is a path to transcendence.

Acceptance and Detachment

This path involves letting go of past wounds and embracing a higher truth. It is about accepting reality as it is and not continuously pining for what we would like it to be—requiring great courage and strength of character to embrace this level of authenticity. Here, detachment is not necessarily being unemotional. It is, in fact, about embracing every emotion we feel and welcoming it without negativity yet being able to observe it with objectivity.

Bhishma's life was a journey of healing through radical acceptance—of his fate, his vows, and his duty. In detaching from his desires, he found a deeper peace, even in the midst of unending loss.

He was born as Devavrata, the beloved son of King Shantanu and the river goddess Ganga. His early years were full of promise, but his life changed when his father fell in love with another woman. Satyavati's father laid down a cruel condition: she could only marry Shantanu if her future children became heirs to the throne. Shantanu was torn, unable to decide between love and duty.

Devavrata made the choice for him. In a moment that would define his life, he renounced his claim to the throne. But it wasn't enough. He then vowed to remain celibate so that no child of his would ever threaten Satyavati's line. That vow gave him his name: Bhishma—the one who took a terrible, fierce vow. It also marked the beginning of his detachment. He gave up his longing for family, love, and legacy, and accepted a life of duty.

But this wasn't a sacrifice made with bitterness. Bhishma's acceptance of his fate became a source of inner strength. He poured his energy into his role as the grandsire of the Kuru dynasty. He protected the kingdom, advised the rulers, and upheld dharma as best he could. His life became an offering. And in that offering, he found a kind of healing—not of the wounds that came from personal loss, but of the soul that seeks meaning through service.

Bhishma's greatest test came during the Kurukshetra war. He stood on the side of the Kauravas, not because he believed in their cause, but because it was his duty to stand by the throne he had sworn to protect. This detachment wasn't coldness. It was a disciplined heart that had learnt to accept pain without turning away from responsibility.

Even in his death, Bhishma practised detachment. Struck down by Arjuna's arrows, he chose not to die immediately. He lay on a bed of arrows for days, waiting for the auspicious moment to leave his body.

In that time, he shared his wisdom with Yudhishthira, offering guidance and clarity. His final act was one of conscious release—a surrender of life itself, free of regret.

Bhishma's healing didn't come from external circumstances changing. It came from within. By embracing his dharma and letting go of personal longing, he found peace. Detachment was not an escape for him. It was his deepest medicine.

Looking Outward

Action-Based Healing

This form of healing comes through doing meaningful work and serving others. Karma yoga reminds us that we are a minuscule part of nature. It tames the ego and teaches humility. If we are willing to introspect, it also brings perspective about our place in this world.

Amrapali's story begins in beauty and longing, but its true power lies in what came after.

Once celebrated as Vaishali's most desired courtesan, she lived amidst wealth, admiration, and the attention of powerful men. Yet the betrayal by King Bimbisara—the man who promised love but left her with heartbreak and humiliation—changed everything.

For a time, grief consumed her. She withdrew from the life that had once defined her. But slowly, something shifted. In the silence of her isolation, she heard the teachings of the Buddha. His words on impermanence, compassion, and non-attachment pierced through her sorrow.

She renounced her worldly life, donating her vast wealth and mango grove to the Sangha. But her healing didn't come through renunciation alone. It was in what she did next.

Amrapali devoted herself to the care of the sick and the destitute. She served the Sangha, tending to the ill, feeding monks, and providing refuge to women abandoned by their families. Her mango grove became a sanctuary, not just for wandering monks but for those in need of compassion and dignity.

This was her karma yoga—selfless service. Each act of care was a balm on her own wounds. In giving to others, she found a way to release the pain of her past. Her beauty, once her identity, became secondary to her work as a healer and benefactor.

In time, she became known not just for her past, but for her deep compassion and wisdom. When she died, it was said she had achieved great spiritual merit, moving towards liberation.

Amrapali's life reminds us that healing is often found not by dwelling on personal loss, but by turning outward, serving where there is need, and letting that service transform us from within.

Healing through Relationships

This path is about healing through love, devotion, or relationships. It might sound counter-intuitive that this path is about returning to the very thing that hurt us. But humans are capable of a wide range of emotions. When one type of relationship is wounded, we can always heal through our many other types of relationships that can be equally, if not more, fulfilling. The Bhakti marga defies logic as it asks us to transcend our limiting beliefs of love and its transactional nature.

A great, enduring example of this is Radha's love and devotion for Krishna. Radha and Krishna's love was unparalleled, but it was never meant to culminate in marriage or worldly union. Krishna, destined for a greater cosmic role, left Vrindavan for Mathura, never to return. He did not reject Radha, but he chose a path beyond personal ties—one of duty, kingship, and ultimately, divinity. This separation could have broken Radha, leaving her lost in grief, but instead, it transformed her.

At first, the pain was unbearable. She wandered through the forests, searching for traces of Krishna, calling out his name. The void he left behind was undeniable. Unlike others, who might have turned to revenge, withdrawal, or new relationships, Radha took an extraordinary path.

Realising that Krishna was never just a mortal lover—he was the divine himself—Radha surrendered her suffering to devotion. Instead of mourning his absence, she turned inward, seeing him everywhere and within herself. This was not detachment in the ascetic sense, but an evolution of love—from a personal attachment to a cosmic connection.

This path of healing looks outward, although it originates in the internal space of one's emotions. Radha expresses her Bhakti openly and with no restraint. Her longing became her strength. She immersed herself in devotion, losing her identity in Krishna's name. Unlike the queens of Krishna's court, who were bound to him in marriage, Radha's connection was eternal, beyond the constraints of worldly relationships. She became a symbol of pure, selfless love, showing that true healing does not always mean forgetting or moving on—it can also mean transforming love into something higher. When heartbreak is surrendered to devotion, it ceases to be suffering and becomes a path to spiritual fulfilment.

I understand that all these examples show characters who chose the path of spirituality by renouncing material life. But healing can happen in parallel with any kind of life path we choose, as long as we are growing in awareness and expanding our consciousness.

A friend tragically lost her two-year-old daughter to the pandemic in 2022. She knew she had to address the grief. She sought help from a grief counsellor while continuing with her corporate job. Then, when she was able to take a sabbatical, she travelled to a retreat in the Himalayas for deeper healing work with guidance from healers there. She returned to her life in the city and started a business. Life's wheels keep turning, and we have got to hold on and keep going with them.

Although the death of a child is life-transforming, it still urges us to go on. And go on, we must. Many of us have responsibilities, commitments, and needs. We have to manage all of them as we tend to our hearts, too. *How* we heal is a choice we can make.

Healing is extremely personal. We each need our unique methods to heal, and we may also need a combination of these types for the healing to work. Some of us need action, some need reflection, some need connection, and some need distance. If you don't know which of these types works for you, it is best to spend time alone and learn to listen to your body and mind on what exactly it needs to restore health and balance.

Whether you choose to go inward or outward, the desire to keep moving forward will ultimately open up the path ahead. As long as we want to heal, the road will appear.

HOW TO CHOOSE A HEALING PATH

But before this, does one need to choose? Yes. It is similar to pursuing a profession or choosing a treatment path for a physical ailment. We get to decide where we are going to focus our energies to heal from trauma.

Everyone heals differently, so how does one decide which path suits them best?

1. Understanding Your Natural Response to Pain

Do you know how you react to discomfort? Do you act, reflect, seek comfort, or detach? Your instinctive response to discomfort holds the clue to your best healing path.

2. Testing Different Modalities

Healing is trial and error. One may say that this is not the time for experimentation. Unfortunately, if we don't know ourselves well enough or have not done this before, then we have to start somewhere. Also, the pain may have been inflicted upon us from outside, but healing is still our responsibility. Finding the right modality for us is sometimes a mix of action, reflection, and connection. Most importantly, we need to be patient with ourselves.

3. Spiritual vs Practical Approaches

Some find peace in spiritual surrender (like Radha did when she chose the path of Bhakti). Others heal through concrete actions (like Sita, who, when exiled to the forest by Rama, devoted herself to raising Luv and Kush with strength and dignity). This is the choice of a God-centric approach or a work-centric pathway. Both are effective as long as we are approaching our healing with awareness and consciousness.

4. External vs Internal Healing

Some heal through service and helping others (karma yoga, charity, and selfless service). Others may need solitude and self-work. This may involve working with a therapist or doing deep sadhana with a spiritual guru to find one's path.

There's no 'one right way' to heal. Whatever works for us and helps us move forward is the best way for us. Explore, adapt, and allow yourself the time to find what truly works for you and your sensibilities.

7

The Physical: Obsession and Addiction in Relationships

Ankita stirred her coffee as she recounted the dream she had the night before.

'I was in a huge amphitheatre. A performance was underway. SRK was on stage—charismatic, larger than life. Everyone was clapping, totally engrossed in the show. But then something strange happened. One by one, people began to leave. No fuss. No drama. Just stood up and walked out. The performance continued, but the seats kept emptying. I was one of the last to leave. I remember looking back at him—still acting, still performing—as I walked away.'

I didn't interrupt. I let the silence linger between us like steam rising from our mugs.

'You're ready,' I finally said.

'Ready for what?'

'To leave the show.'

She looked at me, unsure.

'You've already emotionally checked out of the relationship. That dream was your subconscious playing out what your conscious mind hasn't yet admitted. He'll keep performing—his charm, his drama, his manipulation—but you're done. You're leaving, even if you haven't said it out loud yet.'

She didn't reply, but her face softened. She knew I was right.

What followed between Ankita and Anuj had once felt like destiny. He had walked into her life like he knew exactly which chords to strum. Early on, he was endlessly attentive—checking in on her health, playing the wounded man, asking deep questions about life, karma, and the soul. He told her she was unlike anyone else. He leaned on her emotionally. When legal trouble came his way, she stood by him. She researched case law and even stayed up nights helping him find the right strategy.

He let her in—just enough to keep her invested. But slowly, things began to change.

The Switch

They had spent a quiet evening on a rooftop once, watching the sun set over the city skyline. Ankita had just told him something vulnerable—about how she often felt invisible as a child, how she had learnt to overachieve just to be noticed. Anuj had listened with what seemed like rapt attention. Then, without missing a beat, he had taken her hand and said, 'You never have to perform for me. I see you.'

She had gone home floating, feeling finally understood.

The next day, she texted him something simple: 'Thinking of you. That conversation meant a lot.' No reply.

She waited.

A day passed. Then another. Finally, she sent a longer message, checking in, asking if everything was okay. He responded with, 'I've been swamped with work. Don't overthink.' A few hours later, he posted a selfie with Preeti at a wine-tasting festival.

It became a pattern. Moments of deep connection would be followed by emotional withdrawal. He'd disappear without warning and resurface days later as though nothing had happened. When she brought it up, he would either dismiss her concerns as insecurity or turn the conversation around to how emotionally demanding she was.

She began questioning her own instincts. Was she overreacting? Reading too much into things? Or worse—making him pull away by being too intense?

Still, she stayed. Hoping that the version of him from the rooftop would return and stay for good.

But the honeymoon was over.

Another woman entered the picture—Preeti. At first, Ankita didn't understand what was happening. Anuj started comparing them subtly. He'd say things like, 'Preeti doesn't get as anxious as you,' or 'Preeti has such a calm energy.' The comments stung, but they were wrapped in enough ambiguity that she questioned herself instead.

When Ankita finally gathered the courage to ask where she stood, he went cold. Silent. Aloof. He began withholding affection, or he'd say, 'I already told you I am not in a position to commit till my court cases are resolved.' Ankita would feel guilty for pushing a man who was already under tremendous stress. She'd call to offer support, and he wouldn't pick up. She'd send long messages, only to receive one-word replies. When she pressed for clarity, he made her feel like she was the problem—too emotional, too needy, too intense.

The Fog Inside

There were nights Ankita would sit on the floor of her bedroom, phone in hand, fighting with herself. *Just block him. Cut the cord. You deserve peace.*

She knew what she had to do. The list of offences was long. The pain was undeniable. Her therapist had pointed out the emotional abuse. Her closest friends had started looking at her with quiet concern. But her body wouldn't cooperate.

Her hand hovered over the block button like it was a bomb detonator. Her chest tightened. Her mind played tricks: *What if he finally explains everything? What if you're walking away just before he changes?* Her heart would race. Her stomach would churn. She would put the phone down.

Then pick it up again.

It felt like addiction because it was. The hit of dopamine from even a single message from him was enough to override logic. When he ignored her, she felt like she couldn't breathe. When he returned—even with crumbs—her system would flood with relief. The cycle was chemical. Her nervous system was trapped in a loop of craving and crash.

She read articles about trauma bonds and how intermittent reinforcement was the most powerful psychological hook. But knowing didn't help her escape.

Some nights, she'd manage a full hour of resolve. She would journal, repeat affirmations, and tell herself she deserved better. Then the phone would buzz. A voice note from him. His voice, soft and familiar, would say, 'You crossed my mind today.' And the fog would descend again. Ankita knew it wasn't love but something that had taken its shape. A high that left her lower each time.

One day, after a particularly painful exchange, she asked him directly, 'Why are you treating me this way? Don't I deserve an explanation?'

His response hit like a slap: 'My life is so much at peace without you in it.'

She sat still, stunned. The same man who once said she was his anchor now made her feel like a burden.

But, as reliable as his inconsistency was, even his silence couldn't last long.

A few days later, Anuj messaged again. There was no apology or ownership. Just a casual 'How are you?' as though nothing had happened. When she didn't reply, he sent a voice note reminiscing about the Sunday brunch and her signature pineapple rasam. He was trying to reel her back in.

But something in Ankita had shifted. By then, the dream had shown her the truth. She saw clearly now—he was still on that stage, performing the same role, hoping the audience would return.

She wasn't watching anymore.

OBSESSION AND ENERGY IN RELATIONSHIPS

When love or respect for another becomes an addiction, we lose our autonomy. Like Ankita, we may tie our existence to another, forgetting that our energy is whole within itself.

From a physiological perspective, relationship obsession disrupts our nervous system. The highs of relational passion flood the brain with dopamine, while loss triggers a crash, leading to anxiety and depression.

The heart chakra, the centre of love and connection, becomes blocked, leading to emotional stagnation and a sense of incompleteness. Energetically, cords of attachment keep us bound, making it difficult to move on or reclaim our sense of self.

The story teaches that love, when driven by attachment, enslaves rather than liberates. True love does not demand that we dissolve into another; it allows for connection without loss of self.

Understanding Obsession as an Energetic Force

If you have ever felt trapped in a cycle of craving someone, unable to detach despite knowing the relationship is unhealthy, you have experienced what Ankita felt when she realised the true nature of her dependency on Anuj. Your body and energy field react in ways beyond logic—because obsession is not just an emotional experience; it is chemical, physical, and metaphysical all at once.

Understanding this transaction can bring clarity. Recognising that attachment creates energetic bonds helps us to break free from its debilitating chains. Knowing that obsession alters brain chemistry explains why detachment feels impossible. And most importantly, remembering that love as an addiction is harmful allows us to seek relationships that nourish, rather than consume, our souls.

Obsession masquerading as love is intoxicating. We believe we have found a soulmate, only to realise we are trapped in addiction. It's the modern echo of an ancient tale—that of Rati and Kama.

Rati and Kama Deva: A Tale of Obsession

When we think of the God of love, we think of Kama Deva and his consort Rati, the Goddess of love and desire. They resided in Swarga, the celestial heavens, and could infuse attraction and love in mortals and gods alike. Kama could use his sugarcane bow to send one of his floral arrows zipping into an unsuspecting heart and make it blossom with love and longing.

Together, they wielded immense power. But the story of Rati and Kama is not just one of love; it is a tale of obsession, addiction, and the helpless pull of forces beyond control.

Rati, the goddess of passion and pleasure, was deeply devoted to her consort, Kama—the god of desire. Their love was inseparable, an intoxicating union where pleasure and longing danced endlessly. For Rati, Kama was not just her beloved; he was the source of her vitality, joy, and her very sense of self. Together, they embodied the spark that ignites love in all beings.

But desire can be a dangerous force. When Kama dared to disturb Shiva's deep meditation by firing his arrow of desire, the great ascetic's wrath was swift. In a blaze of fire from his third eye, Shiva incinerated Kama into ashes. In that instant, Rati's world shattered. Without Kama, she was lost. Her vibrant energy dimmed. Her body withered in grief, as if her life force itself had been severed. She wandered in despair, her senses dulled, her heart a hollow void. It was as if her entire being had been emptied. Without him, she believed she was nothing.

Rati pleaded with the gods. She performed penance, withdrew from pleasure, and lived in sorrow, yearning for Kama's return. Her obsession with his absence consumed her. She was trapped in longing, unable to move forward, tethered to a love that had vanished.

Eventually, through her devotion and surrender, the gods took pity. Kama was restored but not in his physical form. He became Ananga, 'the bodiless one', an invisible presence that could stir love without being seen or possessed.

It was then that Rati understood that love could exist without form or ownership. Desire could be felt without being grasped. Her wholeness did not depend on Kama's physical presence but on her ability to hold love within herself. She found balance again—not by clinging, but by releasing. In letting go of her attachment to the body of Kama, Rati reclaimed herself.

Their story became a cosmic lesson: True love is not about possession or obsession. It's about remembering that the source of desire, connection, and joy begins within.

Rati and Kama's tale is not just mythology—it is the story of every soul that the fire of longing has ever burned. It is a reminder that true love is a force of creation, not destruction; a path to wholeness, not dependency.

Is It Love or Lust?

Physical attraction is the silent force that brings people together before a single word is spoken. It can feel fated—an instant recognition, a pull towards someone that defies logic. But what begins as chemistry does not always translate into enduring love. Lust is immediate; it burns hot, feeding on desire and newness. Love, on the other hand, is a slow bloom, revealing itself in moments of vulnerability, trust, and shared understanding.

Physicality does more than initiate a relationship—it shapes how it unfolds and, sometimes, how it ends. At first, passion is all-consuming, a hunger that seems infinite. But bodies, like relationships, evolve. The urgency of touch gives way to a rhythm, a deeper intimacy that is not just about sex but about presence. When this shift does not happen in sync, when one partner remains in the realm of desire while the other seeks comfort in companionship, the disconnect can be sharp.

Sexual compatibility is often underestimated. Too much focus on sex can create a dynamic where love is mistaken for lust, making the relationship feel hollow when the initial passion fades. Too little, and the bond may start to feel like a friendship—secure but missing an essential spark. Add to this the complexity of lust being typically framed as a negative trait. The stereotypes that 'good girls' are not sexual, or that 'cultured' people don't discuss physicality openly, only add to the problem of a basic human desire being brushed under the carpet. All these collectively imposed ideas make it harder for people to talk about their sexual needs with total honesty in relationships.

When two people are misaligned in their desires—one craving closeness through physicality, the other through words or gestures—resentment can build like an unspoken storm.

For some, attraction becomes obsession. The physical becomes the only tether to love, a desperate attempt to keep someone close. But love, real love, is more than bodies meeting in the dark. It is what remains when the fire settles, when touch is not just about wanting but about knowing.

This dynamic between love and lust speaks to the way we express love. For some, the expression is physical and even loud. For others, love is what grows between the spaces that lust leaves behind. It is for the partner to find out if there is love in those crevices or if it is empty. What to do when the physical spark dies? It needs to be addressed. The solutions can come from the couple talking about their needs unhindered. If left unaddressed, the lack of physical affection in a romantic relationship can spell doom for the couple's health in many ways.

PHYSICAL ASPECTS OF RELATIONSHIP BREAKDOWN

When a relationship—of any type—breaks down, it causes stress. The importance we held for that relationship in our hearts determines the extent of stress we feel. The more attached we were to someone, the higher the stress.

Addiction in relationships is not uncommon. There are mothers addicted to children, and vice versa. There are friends addicted to each other. And lovers' addiction, of course, is most recognised. When one person becomes our source of joy, validation, or meaning, our brain responds by releasing chemicals—dopamine, oxytocin, serotonin—that create a loop of dependency with that person and what they offer us. Losing that person is like losing access to those chemicals, triggering symptoms similar to drug withdrawal: anxiety, depression, an inability to focus, and even physical pain.

So, feeling low, losing appetite, and struggling with sleep after a break-up is common, and it is the body's way of telling you that you are, in fact, healthy, with all systems working as they should. But now that you have acknowledged this, how do you break the loop? That is the challenge.

The Slot Machine Analogy

There is a popular analogy to explain addiction to a person: The Slot Machine Analogy. Imagine being at the casino and inserting coins into the slot machine while eagerly waiting for a jackpot. Once in a while, the machine spits out a modest prize. The lure of the big prize is what keeps us hooked. In some of the biggest casinos in Las Vegas, gamblers spend entire nights and days, losing sight of time or even their physiological needs, playing the slot machine while sincerely believing that *this time* they will get lucky. Do they? Someone else always seems to.

Being in an unequal relationship is a lot like this. We wait for the reward: one kind word, a gesture of love, or an act of appreciation to tell us that we are valued. It is the saddest when this sort of addiction happens in a parent–child relationship, where the child is left craving parental attention. They grow to repeat the patterns in their adult relationships until the time they understand this dependency loop and break it once and for all.

We are not chasing the person themselves, but the *feeling* they give us when they finally respond with love or approval—much like a gambler chasing that elusive jackpot high. Here's a quick guide to the brain chemistry when we are in an unhealthy, dependency-led relationship.

When we become addicted to a person in a relationship, our brain undergoes chemical changes similar to substance addiction. Love and emotional attachment activate the brain's reward system, flooding it with neurotransmitters that create feelings of pleasure, security, and craving.

1. Dopamine: The Pleasure Chemical

Falling in love triggers a surge of dopamine, the neurotransmitter associated with pleasure and reward. This creates intense euphoria, similar to the high from drugs like cocaine. Every interaction with the person reinforces this pleasure, making us crave their presence.

2. Oxytocin: The Bonding Hormone

Often called the 'love hormone', oxytocin is released during physical touch, sex, and deep emotional connection. It strengthens trust and bonding, making separation painful. Higher oxytocin levels make us feel safe and attached, reinforcing dependence on the person.

3. Serotonin: The Obsession Factor

Serotonin is the neurotransmitter that helps regulate mood, calmness, and focus. In the initial stages of love, serotonin levels drop, which is similar to what happens in obsessive–compulsive disorder (OCD). This reduction fuels intrusive thoughts and fixation on the person, leading to an inability to focus on anything else.

4. Withdrawal and Cravings

When a relationship ends or there's emotional distance, dopamine levels crash. This mimics withdrawal symptoms seen in drug addiction—leading to anxiety, depression, restlessness, and even physical pain. The brain craves another 'hit' of the person, making detachment difficult.

5. Cortisol and Stress

Emotional rejection or abandonment spikes cortisol, the stress hormone, leading to increased heart rate, anxiety, and a state of emotional turmoil.

Dopamine vs Serotonin: A Tug of War

When dopamine surges (causing euphoria and excitement), serotonin tends to drop. Dopamine drives desire and pursuit, while serotonin stabilises mood. The imbalance creates emotional highs and lows, reinforcing the addictive nature of new love.

Studies show that people in early-stage romantic love have serotonin levels 40 per cent lower than normal—similar to those with OCD. This explains why new lovers experience intrusive thoughts, anxiety, and an inability to focus on anything but the person with whom they are infatuated.

Knowing these chemical reactions helps explain why letting go feels so painful—it's not just emotional, but biological. Recognising this can be the first step in breaking free from unhealthy attachment.

Understanding these physiological changes also lends caution to those who advise their friends to 'just let it go'. It is not that easy to simply let it go. The body, mind, and emotions are all affected in one hot mess. Creating stability in all these parts of our being takes effort, time, and willpower. It is, therefore, necessary to remind ourselves to be kind to the self if we are going through a relationship breakdown, and to be kind to those around us who are facing similar struggles.

- What makes us addicted (dopamine surge, oxytocin, serotonin drop)?
- What makes withdrawal painful (dopamine crash, cortisol spike)?

The cycle of addiction is a push–pull between reward and withdrawal, between the high of connection and the pain of absence.

THE PHYSIOLOGICAL IMPACT

A relationship breakdown triggers deep physiological responses, affecting stress hormones, sleep patterns, and even the immune system. The body perceives emotional loss as a threat, activating survival mechanisms that can take a toll on overall health.

1. Stress Hormones and the Fight-or-Flight Response

When a relationship ends, the brain registers it as a form of social rejection or loss, which spikes cortisol, the body's primary stress hormone. Elevated cortisol levels keep the body in a heightened state of alertness, leading to anxiety, restlessness, and even physical symptoms such as headaches, muscle tension, and digestive issues. Chronic stress can also increase adrenaline, making the heart race and disrupting emotional regulation.

2. Sleep Disturbances and Nervous System Overload

Break-ups often lead to insomnia or disrupted sleep cycles. The nervous system struggles to calm down, causing racing thoughts, nightmares, or early waking. The lack of serotonin (which drops after emotional distress) further reduces melatonin production, making restful sleep difficult. Over time, sleep deprivation worsens emotional resilience, making it harder to heal.

3. Immune System Weakening

Prolonged emotional stress weakens the immune system. Increased cortisol suppresses white blood cell activity, making the body more vulnerable to infections, colds, and inflammation-related conditions. Many people experience fatigue, body aches, and even breakouts after a break-up due to the body's struggle to recover from stress overload.

4. Gut and Appetite Changes

The gut–brain connection means emotional distress can cause digestive problems, loss of appetite, or overeating. Stress can lead to nausea, bloating, or irritable bowel symptoms, while some people turn to food for dopamine-driven comfort eating.

Understanding these physiological effects helps validate the pain of a break-up—it's not just in your head; your body feels it, too.

Now, let's look at certain energetic body aspects that influence us during a relationship breakdown. Yogic philosophy tells us that we have five sheaths. They are: Annamaya Kosha (physical body), Pranamaya Kosha (energy body sheath or vital energy sheath), Manomaya Kosha (mental body sheath), Vijnanamaya Kosha (knowledge or wisdom sheath), and Anandamaya Kosha (bliss sheath).

Relationships and the Pranamaya Kosha

The Pranamaya Kosha—the energetic or vital body—is deeply affected by emotional upheavals, including relationship breakdowns. This layer of our existence governs prana (life force energy) and is intricately linked to breath, emotions, and overall vitality. When a relationship ends, the flow of prana becomes disrupted, leading to various energetic imbalances.

1. Disruptions in Energy Flow

A break-up creates blockages or leaks in prana, particularly in the heart (Anahata) and solar plexus (Manipura) chakras. The heart chakra, responsible for love and connection, may feel heavy, constricted, or depleted, while the solar plexus, which governs personal power and self-worth, may experience instability, nervous tension, or weakness. This often manifests as emotional exhaustion, lack of motivation, or physical tightness in the chest and abdomen.

2. Breath Irregularities and Nervous System Imbalance

Prana is carried through the breath, and emotional distress can lead to shallow, erratic, or constricted breathing. This reduces oxygen flow to the brain, keeping the body in a stressed state of worsening anxiety or grief. We may experience shortness of breath, sighing, or even hold our breath unknowingly, further disrupting the balance of prana.

3. Emotional Residue and Energy Imprints

The Pranamaya Kosha holds energetic imprints of significant past relationships. Every interaction leaves an energetic trace on our prana.

Imagine walking into a room where your ex-partner once sat beside you, and suddenly, you feel a wave of emotion—it could be longing, sadness, or even warmth—without any logical reason. This is the energetic imprint left in your Pranamaya Kosha.

Every interaction, touch, and deep emotional exchange creates a subtle energy imprint in your pranic field. For example, if you and your partner often held hands while talking about your dreams, the energy of that moment lingers in your system. Even after the break-up, certain places, scents, or songs can reactivate these imprints, making you feel their presence energetically, even when they are gone. Imprints that linger create phantom sensations, sudden waves of longing, or a feeling of missing the person's presence energetically.

If not released (or cleansed from our system), these attachments can manifest as chronic fatigue, emotional stagnation, or difficulty moving on. These imprints don't just fade with time—they need conscious release through breathwork, movement, and awareness.

4. Restoring Pranic Balance

To heal the Pranamaya Kosha after a break-up, practices such as pranayama (breathwork), yoga, energy healing, and time in nature help clear stagnant energy, restore balance, and bring emotional and physical vitality back to harmony. The aim is to clear out the residual imprints left on us by the relationship.

CHAKRAS AND ENERGY CORDS: THE INVISIBLE THREADS OF OUR RELATIONSHIPS

Think of your body as more than just flesh and bones. Beneath the surface, there's an energetic system, constantly pulsing, shifting, and responding to the world around you. At the heart of this system are the seven chakras—spinning wheels of energy that store emotions, experiences, and even the residue of past relationships. And then there are energy cords—the unseen threads that bind us to others, for better or worse.

Let's break it down.

1. Root Chakra (Muladhara)—Survival and Stability

Location: Base of the spine

What it governs: Security, grounding, and primal instincts

Relationship impact: A stable relationship makes you feel safe and supported. A toxic one? It triggers insecurity, financial fears, or a deep sense of abandonment. If you've ever felt like you were 'walking on eggshells' around someone, your root chakra took a hit.

2. Sacral Chakra (Svadhisthana)—Emotions and Desire

Location: Just below the navel

What it governs: Passion, creativity, and sensuality

Relationship impact: A passionate, emotionally fulfilling bond lights this chakra up. But betrayal, emotional unavailability, or suppressing your desires can block it, leaving you numb or craving validation in unhealthy ways.

3. Solar Plexus Chakra (Manipura)—Power & Confidence

Location: Upper abdomen (just above the navel)

What it governs: Self-worth, personal power, and decision-making

Relationship impact: A relationship that empowers you makes this chakra shine. But control, manipulation, or being in a one-sided dynamic? That drains it, leaving you second-guessing yourself or feeling trapped. Ever lost yourself in a relationship? That's your solar plexus energy dimming.

4. Heart Chakra (Anahata)—Love and Connection

Location: Centre of the chest

What it governs: Love, empathy, and emotional balance

Relationship impact: Love flows freely when this chakra is open. But heartbreak, grief, or unreciprocated feelings create blockages, making it hard to trust or open up again. If you've ever felt like you can't move on from someone, their energy may still be lodged here.

5. Throat Chakra (Vishuddha)—Communication and Truth

Location: Throat area

What it governs: Expression, honesty, and speaking your truth

Relationship impact: A healthy relationship encourages open, honest conversations. But if you've been silenced, gaslit, or forced to suppress your needs, this chakra tightens—literally. Ever had a lump in your throat during an argument? That's blocked energy.

6. Third Eye Chakra (Ajna)—Intuition and Perception

Location: Between the eyebrows

What it governs: Inner wisdom, foresight, and clarity

Relationship impact: When you're in tune with your intuition, you can see things for what they are. But if someone constantly lies to you, dismisses your gut feelings, or makes you doubt yourself, this chakra gets clouded. That's why so many people say, *'I should have seen the red flags'*—but their third eye was muddled at the time.

7. Crown Chakra (Sahasrara)—Spiritual Connection and Higher Purpose

Location: Top of the head

What it governs: Spirituality, enlightenment, and universal connection

Relationship impact: Some relationships elevate your soul, while others make you feel disconnected from your higher self. If you've ever felt like you 'lost yourself' in a toxic dynamic, your crown chakra may have been cut off from its source.

Energy Cords: The Unseen Ties That Bind Us

Now, here's where it gets even more interesting. Every deep relationship—whether romantic, familial, or platonic—creates energetic cords between you and the other person. These cords act like invisible bridges, transferring emotions, thoughts, and energy.

- Healthy cords feel light and nourishing, like an open channel of love and support.
- Toxic cords feel heavy, draining, and intrusive—keeping you mentally stuck in a relationship long after it's ended.

Have you ever struggled to stop thinking about an ex? Or felt exhausted just by being near someone? That's the power of energetic cords at work. The good news? These cords can be strengthened, cleared, or cut, depending on what serves your highest good.

Understanding your chakras and energy cords hands you the power to navigate relationships with awareness. Instead of being pulled around by emotional chaos, you start to recognise the patterns: What uplifts you, what depletes you, and most importantly, how to reclaim your energy from an unhealthy place.

Love isn't just about who we hold in our arms; it's also about the energy we possess within ourselves.

How Energy Cords Form in Relationships

Every meaningful relationship we form creates energy cords, invisible threads that connect us to another person. Some cords are nourishing, strengthening our chakras and overall energy, while others are draining, leaving us feeling depleted or stuck. Let's look at two examples—one healthy and one toxic—to understand how these cords work.

A Healthy Relationship with Two Strong Cords: Meera and Arjun (Love and Support)

Meera and Arjun have been together for five years. They respect each other's space, encourage one another's growth, and communicate openly. Their relationship has formed two strong energy cords:

1. Heart Chakra Cord (Anahata—Love and Emotional Connection)

Meera and Arjun share a deep emotional bond based on trust, respect, and care. Their heart chakra cord is balanced, allowing love to flow freely. They feel safe expressing their emotions without fear of judgement. If one of them has a rough day, the other intuitively senses it, offering support without being overbearing.

2. Throat Chakra Cord (Vishuddha—Honest Communication)

They communicate openly, even about difficult topics. This throat chakra cord keeps their energy clear and open by catching misunderstandings or rising resentments before they get out of control. If one of them is upset, they feel comfortable discussing it instead of suppressing emotions.

Meera and Arjun's energy exchange is mutually enriching. Their connection leaves them feeling uplifted, secure, and inspired. Even when apart, they feel at peace because their cords are light and healthy.

A Toxic Relationship with Multiple Draining Cords: Reema and Kabir (Obsession and Emotional Manipulation)

Reema and Kabir have been in an on-and-off relationship for two years. Kabir is emotionally unavailable, yet he keeps Reema hooked with occasional affection. Reema, on the other hand, finds it impossible to let go despite feeling drained. Their connection has formed multiple toxic cords:

1. Solar Plexus Chakra Cord (Manipura—Power and Control)

Kabir constantly makes Reema feel unworthy and desperate for his approval. This solar plexus cord is imbalanced, leaving Reema doubting herself and feeling powerless. When Kabir ignores her, she feels anxious. When he gives her attention, she experiences a temporary high—almost like an addiction.

2. Sacral Chakra Cord (Svadhisthana—Desire and Attachment)

Their physical intimacy has created a deep, energetic bond, but it's not based on a genuine emotional connection. The sacral chakra cord is dense and tangled, making it difficult for Reema to detach. Even when she tries to move on, she feels pulled back as if something is incomplete.

3. Third Eye Chakra Cord (Ajna—Confusion and Illusions)

Kabir gaslights Reema, making her question her own intuition. This third-eye chakra cord is clouded, preventing Reema from seeing the reality of the relationship. She feels trapped in a loop, unable to trust her instincts about walking away.

Reema's energy is constantly being drained. Her emotions swing between hope and despair, and she feels exhausted even when she's not around Kabir. Their cords are imbalanced, keeping her stuck in a cycle of emotional dependency.

Chakra Clearing: When and How to Do It

Energy cords don't just disappear when a relationship ends. If a connection was deep, its energetic residue lingers in your system, sometimes for years. This is where chakra clearing comes in.

What Is Chakra Clearing?

It's the process of releasing stagnant energy, cutting unhealthy cords, and restoring balance to your chakras. This can be done through:

- Meditation and visualisation (imagining the cords dissolving)

- Breathwork and movement (yoga, dancing, or exercise)
- Energy healing (Reiki, Pranic Healing, or crystal therapy)
- Sound therapy (mantras, singing bowls)
- Conscious detachment (acknowledging the past but no longer feeding it energy)

When Should You Do It?

- After a break-up or an emotionally heavy relationship
- If you feel stuck in the past or constantly think about someone
- You sense draining or toxic energy from certain people
- If you feel emotionally exhausted without a clear reason
- You want to clear space for new relationships

Not every cord needs to be cut; some just require rebalancing. Healthy relationships leave light, uplifting imprints. But it's time to leave those that weigh you down and clear that energy to reclaim your power.

Our relationships shape our energy in ways we don't always see, but we can always feel them. When we become aware of these energetic ties, we gain the power to nurture the good, release the bad, and protect our energy. At the end of the day, your energy is yours alone, and you get to decide who has access to it.

You are the keeper of your energy. The more you protect it, the more it protects you.

8

Karmic Relationships: Twin Flame Connections and Soul Contracts

Have you ever felt like you were destined to meet someone, only to have the relationship break you open? This chapter is for you.

This is a powerful modern-day 'twin flame' story. I use the term 'twin flames' here for convenience—to describe a pattern of relationships marked by intense metaphysical connections. While 'twin flames' is often used interchangeably with soulmates or karmic ties, each follows distinct patterns, which I have outlined in this chapter. Additionally, these connections are not exclusive to romance; they can occur between people in any type of relationship.

Marina Abramović and Ulay, both performance artists from Serbia, are famous in the global art world. In 2010, Marina presented her most ambitious work, titled 'The Artist Is Present', at the Museum of Modern Art in New York. It was a live performance in which the audience was invited to take turns sitting across from Marina at a table and being present without exchanging words. Visitors waited for hours to participate in this unique experience, locking eyes with the performance art icon in an unscripted, silent exchange.

Marina received a surprise that day. Her former lover, Ulay, whom she had not seen for over twenty-two years, casually walked to the table, and sat across from her, creating an unscripted, raw emotional moment that brought tears to anyone who witnessed it. The video went viral on social media.

Marina and Ulay's love story mirrors what's known as the twin flame journey: A deeply karmic entanglement of two souls who meet again and again across lifetimes until their lessons are learnt.

Marina and Ulay first met in 1976 as fire meets air—recognising each other in a way that defied logic. It was not love at first sight but something deeper, something older. A knowing. As if their souls had conspired long before their bodies arrived.

Together, they became one breath, one force. Both pursuing a creative life, they used this potent energy in their work to highlight issues of gender, ego, and identity. They pushed, pulled, collided, and merged, erasing creative boundaries between man and woman, artist, and art. All their performances were rituals—acts of trust and surrender that demanded more than mere devotion.

They lived in a van, abandoned their names, and forged a new self: a shared existence they called The Other (created by their merging). But the more they dissolved into each other, the more their own edges frayed.

They would sit motionless for hours, eyes locked, daring the other to break first. They would tie their hair together and sit back-to-back till they could endure it. They would plug their noses and breathe into each other's mouths until their lungs ran out of oxygen, and they collapsed. It was a slow unravelling, a beauty that could not be sustained.

The couple decided to marry. This, too, was to be artistic—and a tad dramatic at that. They wrote to the Chinese government for permission to walk the length of the Great Wall of China from opposite ends so they could meet in the middle and get married. They waited seven years for approval. By then, their relationship had deteriorated. It could not sustain the intensity of the demands upon them. When they received permission from China, they decided to do the 2,500-km walk anyway, staying at inns along the way for over ninety days.

They sent messages through their translators. Somewhere along this journey, Ulay impregnated his Chinese translator. When Marina learnt of this, she was heartbroken. What was meant to be a wedding became a goodbye when they finally met in the middle of the Great Wall. With a final embrace, they let go.

Decades passed before their silent reunion at MoMA. That moment across the table was an unspoken acknowledgement of love, pain, and the passage of time. When their eyes met, tears broke the dam of time. Twin flames do not always burn forever. But their fire leaves an imprint that never fades.

TWIN FLAMES

When discussing the metaphysical aspects of relationships, it is essential to address twin flame connections. It is only in the past few decades, owing to an explosion of social media content about twin flames, that we are able to recognise and name certain relationships as such.

Ulay and Marina's story perfectly encapsulates the many stages of a twin flame journey—intense connection, painful separation, and individual evolution. Twin flame relationships trigger us to embark on a deeper spiritual path. Almost always, if it is a twin flame connection, both partners will be led to greater awareness and awakening. It could be a spiritual journey or the process of expanding one's awareness and understanding of life.

In twin flame connections, two souls are deeply intertwined, mirroring each other's strengths and wounds, inevitably drawn together yet often torn apart until both have evolved to their highest potential.

What Is a Twin Flame?

A twin flame is not just a soulmate—it is the other half of your soul. Unlike soulmates, who bring comfort and harmony, twin flames challenge and dismantle. They hold up a mirror to your deepest fears and unresolved traumas, forcing you to confront them. While this connection is deeply spiritual and transformative, it is not always smooth or romantic. In fact, it is often tumultuous, filled with cycles of attraction and repulsion until both individuals reach a place of balance and self-realisation.

The purpose of a twin flame relationship is not just to be together, but to awaken each other, triggering deep healing and personal evolution. This is why twin flame unions are often intense, overwhelming, and, oftentimes, painful. There is hardly a twin flame relationship that is smooth.

The Stages of a Twin Flame Connection

A twin flame journey unfolds in distinct stages, mirroring the cycles of growth and transformation.

1. Recognition and Awakening

The first meeting is electrifying. There is an immediate sense of familiarity, a knowing that defies logic. The connection is magnetic, and both individuals are drawn together with an intensity that feels fated.

2. The Honeymoon Phase

In the initial stages, the connection feels euphoric. There is an overwhelming sense of unity, as if you have found the missing piece of your soul. This phase is filled with deep conversations, intense emotions, and an almost telepathic connection.

3. The Mirror Stage

As the euphoria fades, unresolved wounds begin to surface. The twin flame mirrors your deepest fears, insecurities, and past traumas. This is where conflicts arise, often leading to emotional turmoil.

4. The Runner and Chaser Dynamic

One person—usually the one more spiritually evolved—becomes the chaser, desperately seeking union. The other, overwhelmed by the intensity, becomes the runner, pulling away to avoid the emotional chaos. The separation can be heartbreaking, leaving both individuals in deep distress.

5. Surrender and Transformation

During separation, both twins are forced into deep self-work. This period is crucial for individual healing and growth. The focus shifts from external validation to internal self-discovery. Only when both have reached a place of self-love and wholeness can reunion become possible.

6. Harmonisation and Reunion

Once both twins have evolved, the energy between them shifts. They reunite in a higher state of consciousness, no longer dependent on each other for completion but coming together as equals, just as Shiva and Parvati did.

The Twin Flame Journey of Shiva and Parvati

Hindus often cite the love story of Shiva and Parvati as eternal and ideal—a goal to strive for. But their journey is not one of effortless love. It is a tale of separation, yearning, self-transformation, and eventual union—much of it marked by ascetic withdrawal, rejection, trials, and an ultimate merging of divine energies. Unlike the sanitised versions that share a limited understanding of their relationship as one of celestial romance, the ancient texts depict a far more complex dynamic: The meeting of two vastly different souls, clashing, evolving, and finally harmonising.

Separation and Individual Growth

Before Parvati, there was Sati—the woman who first loved Shiva. The daughter of Prajapati Daksha, Sati was drawn to Shiva's austere, otherworldly existence. She defied her father's wishes and married the ascetic god, only to find herself trapped between the two most dominant forces in her life: Her love for Shiva and her father's hostility towards him. Daksha, furious that his daughter had married a deity who smeared himself with ash and wore a garland of skulls, deliberately excluded Shiva from a grand yajna (sacrificial ceremony). Sati, consumed by humiliation and grief, walked into the fire and immolated herself.

Sati's death plunged Shiva into an abyss of mourning. He withdrew from the world, retreating into the Himalayas, shutting out everything, including destiny itself. This marks the first great separation in their journey—one lover consumed by grief, the other reincarnated to try again.

Parvati was born with a purpose—to reunite with Shiva. But she was not yet his equal. A mortal princess, raised in luxury and comfort, she was everything Shiva was not. Yet, she remembered. Something within her knew that her soul was bound to his. When she came of age, she sought him out, only to find a man utterly indifferent to her presence. He had seen the fleeting nature of the material world and wanted no part in it. Love, to him, was an illusion, a distraction from the path of liberation.

Parvati's rejection by Shiva only strengthened her determination. She abandoned her royal comforts and embraced the ascetic path. She lived in the forests, performed severe penances, and meditated for years, all with the goal of matching Shiva's energy. She fasted, endured the elements, and burned away her identity as a princess, emerging as a yogini, someone worthy of standing beside him. It was only then that Shiva opened his eyes.

Ego, Surrender, and Divine Tests

Shiva, however, was not yet ready to accept her. He decided to test her resolve. According to some texts, he appeared before her in disguise, ridiculing himself, warning her against marrying a god who smeared himself in ash and wandered among corpses. Parvati, unwavering in her devotion, dismissed these taunts. She had seen beyond his exterior; she knew his essence.

Yet surrender was needed from both sides. Just as Parvati had to strip away her identity as a princess, Shiva had to relinquish his detachment and acknowledge the human experience of love. It was Vishnu who intervened, reminding Shiva that his role was not just to destroy but also to participate in the cycle of creation. And so, reluctantly, Shiva agreed to the union.

Shiva's surrender to the union with Parvati reflects a critical twin flame lesson: Love must exist beyond desire, beyond attachment, and in its purest essence.

Harmonisation of Opposites

In fairy-tales, folk tales, and even in real life, marriage is portrayed as the desirable happy conclusion. But Shiva and Parvati's marriage was not an end but the beginning of another trial. Much like any couple with incompatibility issues, Shiva and Parvati were pulled in opposite directions. They represented opposite forces—destruction and creation, detachment and devotion, stillness and action.

Their early days together were riddled with friction. Parvati wanted companionship; Shiva was accustomed to solitude. She longed for a home; he roamed among the mountains. She desired engagement; he lost himself in meditation. They loved each other, but they struggled to align. Think of a man who withdraws and the woman who wonders what happened. Even the gods are not immune to this phenomenon of one partner pulling away and the other left with the choice of chasing or finding a different path.

In this case, Parvati, refusing to be a mere shadow of Shiva, withdrew and performed another set of austerities to transform into her higher self—Adi Shakti, the primordial energy of the universe. In this form, she was not just Shiva's consort but his equal.

This is the essence of the twin flame journey: Both must evolve individually before they can truly merge.

It was through her transformation that the true balance between the couple was struck. She channelled his destructive force into creative power, softening his edges without diminishing his essence. He, in turn, learnt to remain engaged in the world without losing his transcendental nature. Their union resulted in the birth of Kartikeya, the warrior god who would go on to destroy the demon Tarakasura—an embodiment of the darkness that had once threatened the cosmic order.

The Eternal Dance

Shiva and Parvati's story does not end with their union. It is a cycle of separation, transformation, and reunion that is repeated over cosmic ages. When Parvati takes the form of Kali, losing herself in unbridled fury, Shiva must lie beneath her feet to restore balance. When Shiva wanders into deep asceticism, Parvati must remind him of the material world's role in the divine play. Their love is not static; it is a dance, a continuous push and pull of energies, forever seeking equilibrium. Aren't most relationships a reflection of this push-pull?

Unlike karmic relationships, which burn out once lessons are learnt, or soulmate bonds, which offer comfort and ease, twin flame relationships are forged in fire, destruction, and rebirth. They demand dissolution of the ego, deep transformation, and the ability to hold space for chaos and creation alike. Shiva and Parvati's journey embodies the highest expression of such a union—not perfect, not easy, but undeniably cosmic in its scale.

Their story is not one of effortless love, but of love that endures, evolves, and transcends—the essence of a true twin-flame connection.

What Happens Energetically during the Separation of Twin Flames?

Separation is not just a physical distance—it is an energetic shift. Twin flames share an energetic cord, and when they separate, the disconnection can feel like withdrawal. This is why many experience physical symptoms such as exhaustion, heart palpitations, or even unexplained sadness.

Energetically, one or both twins undergo a dark night of the soul—a period of intense emotional and spiritual upheaval that forces them to shed old patterns and false identities. This phase is critical because it prepares them for eventual reunion.

Why Do Twin Flames Go through Cycles of Separation and Reunion?

Twin flame relationships are about evolution. If both individuals are not at the same vibrational frequency, they will be pulled apart. This is not punishment—it is the universe's way of ensuring that both do the necessary inner work.

Reunion happens when both twins have reached a level of spiritual maturity where they no longer need each other but choose to be together. Until then, the cycle continues, forcing growth with each separation.

In many ways, the twin flame journey is not about union with the other but about reunion with oneself. Only when you have faced your own shadows, healed your wounds, and stepped into your power can true union with your twin flame take place. Just as Parvati had to transform herself before Shiva could recognise her as his equal, twin flames must undergo their own metamorphosis before they can truly come together.

The journey is arduous but also profoundly sacred. It is not about finding love in another, but about discovering the love and divinity within yourself. That is the true essence of the twin-flame connection.

SOUL CONTRACTS

I was first introduced to the concept of soul contracts when I was learning how to read an astrology chart. My understanding of the dance of destiny and willpower became more pronounced through the study of soul contracts.

Simply put, soul contracts are agreements that our soul makes to undergo certain life experiences that it believes will get us closer to liberation from the cycle of birth and death. (Liberation refers to moksha or freedom from repeated births and deaths.) For believers in reincarnation, soul contracts make for a fascinating explanation for why we are born to a specific set of parents, in a specific environment, meet certain people, and undergo experiences—all for a course that our soul has enrolled us in so that we become better students of life.

If we understand our life experiences and relationships as soul contracts, then the lessons we are here to learn are fairly easy to identify. Is it a lesson about money management, attachment to people or things, learning to break certain relationship patterns, or learning to be independent? The lessons emerge throughout life.

In the context of relationships, the soul contract suggests that our souls have already predetermined whom we will meet, as well as the intensity and outcome of those relationships. Our free will rests in how quickly we learn our lesson from that relationship, or maintain it over the long term, as the case may be. The challenge for us is to identify whether this relationship is for keeps or is a passing lesson.

Ancestral Karma in Relationships

We have soul contracts with every important relationship in our life: Parents, siblings, best friends, extended relations, teachers, and people of importance that we interact with regularly. Soul contracts are usually drawn up within the framework of our ancestral karma. In modern psychology parlance, this is referred to as generational trauma. We are all part of an ancestral line—two lines, actually, maternal and paternal. Studies show how unresolved relationship patterns tend to repeat in subsequent generations till they are healed and released from the ancestry completely.

The unhealed issues can be about abandonment, abuse, addiction, or personality traits that are debilitating. For example, in an ancestry, a woman who was excommunicated from her family line and village several generations ago for being an unwed mother may repeat that energy in a niece two generations later. This gives the ancestral line another opportunity to, this time, support the pregnant woman rather than abandon her, thereby healing the past trauma.

Identification and healing of such patterns are done through various modalities, one of them specific to family systems, called 'Systemic Constellations', introduced in modern psychology group therapy by Bert Hellinger, a German war hero turned priest. Systemic Constellations combine elements of Transactional Analysis and energy healing to identify and resolve past traumas within family lines.

Across cultures, different traditions offer ways to resolve ancestral karma. When I was visiting villages in Vietnam, I saw small decorative shrines built by the front gate. In a cubby hole of this decorative spirit house, the villagers kept a bowl of water and some food. This was for the passing ancestral spirits so they could rest a while and be refreshed before continuing their journey. Also, if the spirits visited the village home, they should always be welcomed with drinks and food.

Within Shamanic healing work, there are several healers dedicated to ancestral karma clearing. The Vedic knowledge system lays out specific rituals to appease the *Pitrus* (ancestors). This can be through the new moon (Amavasya) rituals of offering Tarpanam. And the widely practised rituals during Pitru Paksha—the fortnight of the ancestors—when it is believed that the ancestors are more accessible to us; rituals performed during this fortnight serve as a general tonic to remember them. The fortnight culminates in the Mahalaya Amavasya, the new moon dedicated to the Pitrus.

Karmic Relationships

All important relationships are soul contracts. Some of these soul-contract relationships are karmic in nature. The general understanding of karmic relationships is that they are romantic past-life connections that we encounter again to complete the love story. But karmic relationships are far from romantic.

Karmic relationships are often torturous connections that leave us drained and with many lessons to learn. The primary purpose of a karmic relationship is to give us yet another opportunity to break a relationship pattern. This pattern is often one that's perpetuated in our ancestral line, or it is one that we have carried as part of our karma to clear. Regardless of how it manifests in our lives, it is an intense relationship that leaves a profound impact on us.

Here are some characteristics that will help you identify a karmic relationship:

1. Instant Magnetism with a Heavy Energy

Karmic relationships often start with an intense attraction, but the energy feels chaotic, overwhelming, or even addictive rather than clear and balanced.

2. Repetitive Painful Patterns

The relationship follows cycles of highs and lows, often repeating the same conflicts, misunderstandings, or toxic patterns, leaving both individuals drained rather than evolved.

3. Strong Emotional Triggers

Karmic partners bring out deep insecurities, fears, and wounds from past lives or childhood. The relationship feels like an emotional battlefield rather than a space of mutual growth.

4. Unresolved Power Struggles

There is often a theme of control, dependency, or manipulation. One person may feel trapped in the relationship, yet unable to break free due to emotional, financial, or psychological entanglement.

5. Destined to End

Karmic relationships rarely last in the long run. Their purpose is to teach a lesson, and once learnt, the relationship dissolves. This could take anywhere between a few weeks to a lifetime, depending on how soon the partners learn their lessons and move on.

6. Lack of Spiritual Alignment

While karmic partners may be drawn together by fate, their personal growth paths do not align. They struggle to evolve together, often keeping each other stuck rather than progressing spiritually.

7. Toxic Dependency Instead of Growth

Karmic relationships often create codependency, where one or both partners feel they *need* the other rather than growing into their highest selves independently.

8. Feeling 'Owed' or Incomplete Until It Ends

There's a sense of karmic debt, as if something needs to be repaid from a past life. One or both partners might feel obligated to stay, even when they know it's unhealthy.

Nagaratna was in an abusive marriage with a chronic alcoholic. He not only drank every evening till he lost total control of his senses, but he would also come home and beat Nagaratna. I met Nagaratna a couple of years after her husband had succumbed to his excessive drinking. She told me that the beating all those years had been unbearable. She had learnt to use the brace position when he was hitting her senseless.

When I asked her why she didn't leave earlier, she had no clear answer. She was under the same societal pressure that anyone in a difficult marriage faces. She had a young son who would soon grow up to understand what was happening. He would ask questions, and it would be dangerous to make a model of the husband's behaviour for her son. She was financially independent and could leave if she wanted to. But she couldn't—or rather, she wouldn't.

She had to work through the psychological entanglement that kept her tethered to a wife-beating alcoholic and summon all her courage before she could finally walk out with her son. Her lesson was to find her strength and use it. The relationship was telling her to break the pattern of staying in unhealthy dynamics out of fear or a sense of obligation.

Karmic relationships run deep in family ties, too. They are perhaps more difficult to break because of social and mental conditioning.

Anand, now 53, was raised by a father who was impossible to please. No matter how well he performed in school, how obedient he was, or how hard he worked in the family business, his father always managed to find a flaw. There was always something more Anand should have done, something at which he had failed. The parental approval Anand sought never came.

When he was old enough to make his own choices, he turned away from the family business and pursued a corporate job in another city. This was a big turning point in his life, no doubt. Distance gave him relief, but the emotional grip remained. Every decision he made carried the shadow of his father's judgement. Even as a successful professional, he felt undeserving of success. At times, he caught himself doubting his own decisions, as though he needed his father's approval—even when his father wasn't around.

When I asked him why he still sought validation from a man who never gave it, he hesitated. 'I don't know, but he's my father,' he admitted. 'It's like I owe him something.'

Through deep introspection, Anand realised his father's criticism mirrored an unfinished karmic debt. The relationship was perhaps meant to teach him self-worth, independent of external validation. The lesson was clear: he had to stop seeking permission to be enough. The karmic bond wasn't about pleasing his father—it was about learning to stand tall, knowing his worth without needing anyone else to confirm it.

Here's how to distinguish between twin flames, karmic relationships, and soulmates:

Aspect	Twin Flames	Karmic Relationships	Soulmates
Purpose	Help you grow by reflecting your deepest self	Teach difficult lessons and clear past karma	Offer love, support, and companionship
Intensity	Deep, transformative, and often challenging	Toxic, repetitive, and full of drama	Peaceful, natural, and nurturing
Longevity	May separate and reunite, but personal growth is the goal	End once the lesson is learnt	Can last a lifetime
Energy Exchange	Share an intense, telepathic connection	Feel draining and exhausting	Feel balanced and uplifting
Lesson	Teach self-love and spiritual awakening	Teach boundaries and self-worth	Teach trust, companionship, and mutual growth

THE AFTERMATH OF BREAKING A SPIRITUAL CONNECTION

You have identified the spiritual connection. Now what?

Recognising a twin flame, karmic relationship, or soulmate connection is just the beginning. The real challenge lies in understanding what to do with this awareness. When such relationships end—especially a twin flame or a deep soul contract—the effects go far beyond the emotional. There are metaphysical consequences that ripple through your energy field, your subconscious, and your very sense of self.

The Metaphysical Consequences of Breaking a Soul Contract

Ending a soul contract, whether by choice or circumstance, is not just about cutting ties—it's about dissolving an agreement that was meant to teach a lesson. In the case of a twin flame, the separation is often excruciating because the bond is energetic, not just emotional. You may feel a sudden emptiness, as if a part of you is missing. Some experience physical symptoms—fatigue, headaches, or even unexplained aches—as the body processes the energetic shift.

The separation can also trigger a deep spiritual awakening. Twin flames are meant to accelerate growth, and breaking the bond often forces one or both individuals to confront their deepest fears, wounds, and unresolved karmic patterns. The pain serves as a catalyst, pushing you to evolve in ways you wouldn't have otherwise.

Karmic relationships, on the other hand, leave behind a different kind of energy. When you break free from a karmic bond, it can feel like releasing a heavy weight. There is often relief, even if the ending is painful, because the relationship was built on unresolved past-life energies that were never meant to last. However, if the lesson isn't fully learnt, the cycle may repeat in another form—either with the same person or through a different relationship carrying the same patterns.

Soulmate bonds, being more harmonious, tend to dissolve with mutual acceptance when they have run their course. The energetic shift is gentler, with a sense of gratitude for the connection rather than deep turmoil.

How Energetic Shifts Occur Post-Separation

When a deep spiritual bond breaks, the energy fields of both individuals undergo a significant transformation. The most noticeable shift is in the heart and sacral chakras—the centres of love and emotional connection. If the separation is traumatic, these chakras may become blocked, leading to feelings of emotional numbness or difficulty in forming new connections.

For twin flames, the separation often triggers a 'dark night of the soul', where one or both individuals experience intense loneliness, confusion, and existential questioning. This is because twin flames mirror each other's wounds, and separation forces both to heal independently before they can align with their higher purpose.

Energetically, the separation initiates a recalibration. Over time, as healing occurs, the blocked energy releases, allowing for personal growth and transformation. If the bond was truly a twin flame connection, reunion is possible, but only after both individuals have evolved beyond their past wounds.

The key to moving forward is surrender—trusting that the separation serves a higher purpose. Whether the relationship returns or not, the spiritual growth it sparks is what truly matters.

9

Trust the Timing: Why Every Healing Journey Is Unique

A sharp scream pierced the forest air. The birds squawked in protest.

Adesh's confident, masculine, always-in-control aura had slipped from its tall pedestal. Varsha flinched, almost dropping her book. The culprit was a spider.

She saw Adesh giggle nervously. She smiled politely but noticed everything: How Adesh's energy carried accents of fear when the forest went dark, the way his hand hovered near his phone like a crutch against the rawness of the natural environment, how he kept corporate office timings even when the day gave him the freedom to surrender and flow as he pleased.

She watched him swat a mosquito, then grumble about wanting to shower. 'There's no hot water here?' he asked, voice half-joking, half-annoyed. The joke of someone who had never once truly unplugged. He wore a cotton kurta and trousers, but they were freshly ironed. His backpack was leather. 'Basic. Very basic,' he said a tad too loudly over the phone to someone enquiring about the accommodation. It was the tone of a man steeped in luxury but talked austerity.

And when they finally sat for silence, the sacred hush Varsha loved—the kind that wrapped the trees in velvet—he instantly filled it with his out-of-tune humming. Every few seconds, he shifted to another song fragment: nothing coherent, just enough to break the stillness. Just enough to avoid the unbearable sound of his own thoughts catching up to him.

She had once believed this man loved nature. He spoke of forests with reverence, of silence as a teacher, of solitude as a path. But here, surrounded by real trees, real dirt, and real creatures, he was exposed.

Adesh was terrified of stillness. And silence. And spiders. And maybe even her.

That was the first fracture: The moment when the performance began to slide.

They had met at a spirituality conference years ago. He had given a talk on 'The Disappearing Self'. It was full of metaphors—rivers returning to oceans and salt dolls dissolving into water. She remembered being struck by the quiet confidence in his voice, the deliberate pace of his words, the way he seemed to command the room without asking for it.

Later, he messaged her on social media. He said her question during the Q&A had stayed with him. They began exchanging thoughts on detachment, art, karma, and death. She was sceptical at first. But he was persistent—not in a pushy way, at least not yet—but with a steady stream of care: A poem here, a compliment there, reflections on non-duality, Rilke, tantric surrender. 'You are a rare one,' he once wrote. 'A forest mind in a city world.'

It felt special. Like finding someone who could meet her at the level of soul.

Over the years, their exchanges deepened. He became her first reader, idea-bouncer, and the man who 'saw' her creative fire and encouraged it. Except, the encouragement came with strings. She owed him, didn't she? That was the trick. He made her feel like everything he gave her—time, attention, even silence—was a debt.

'You only write when you're not in survival mode,' he once said. 'Maybe that's why your work is so raw. Suffering keeps you sharp.'

She had thought it was insight. Now, she wonders if it was envy.

When she shared her reverent forest poem—the one about the trees listening—his reply had been a parody:

The leaf fell.
Big deal.
A beetle moved.
Must mean something.
The tree creaked.
Ah! The gods have spoken.
Another poem done.

It hit like a slap disguised as wit. She brushed it off at first, explaining it away as teasing, his attempt to make her tougher. Until she sent him another poem—this one rooted in her years of studying astrology:

Venus in Capricorn speaks of commitment.
A slow-growing love, rooted like an oak.
Mars there smoulders,
And Saturn watches with solemn patience.
This is no fling.
This is stone meeting bone,
This is time.

His reply?

> I swallowed the cosmos last night.
> Mars sizzled down my spine.
> Venus perched between my thighs.
> Saturn spanked me for forgetting foreplay.
> By morning, I was galaxies lighter.
> A new kind of yoga.

She sat staring at the message—not laughing, not even angry. Just stunned. It wasn't just a dirty joke. It was contamination. He had twisted her sacred into spectacle, her wisdom into innuendo, her devotion into a setup for his ego. But even then, she hesitated to call it what it was: Emotional manipulation. Grooming. Misuse of intimacy.

Every time Varsha found clarity—about her vision, her work, the structure she needed to build a life of purpose—he would mock it. He romanticised aimlessness, paraded confusion as freedom, and called it 'living fully'. He scoffed at direction, quoting Krishna out of context to justify his own lack of discipline. Draped in a saffron shawl, he postured as a spiritual guide, misrepresenting mythology to sound enlightened while barely scratching its surface.

When Varsha set emotional boundaries, he pushed them. When she resisted his inappropriate touch, he acted wounded, as though her resistance was betrayal after all he had 'done' for her. He called it 'play', 'freedom', 'high philosophy'. But it wasn't. It was entitlement: A man cloaking infidelity in spiritual jargon while his wife remained unaware of the quiet trespasses he committed every day.

This wasn't expansion. It was erosion of clarity, dignity, and trust. His visit to the forest crystallised it all for Varsha.

He commented on her routines like they were curiosities. 'You're still doing puja every evening? You know, that kind of discipline is . . . sweet. But maybe it's just another mask?'

He touched her back too often, letting his hand linger just long enough for her to freeze. He joked about his affection spiking for her, infantilising the air between them with baby talk, making himself seem non-threatening while forcing her to drop her guard further.

When she pulled away, he sulked, pretending to be occupied with something grandly philosophical. That night, she stepped out alone to sit on a rock beneath the pongamia tree. The stars above her were sharp, loud with clarity.

She saw it all clearly now: How he had needed her to feel grateful so he could feel powerful, how he had inserted himself into her creativity then subtly undermined it, how he had turned her spiritual fire into his private stage.

She had mistaken intensity for intimacy, language for truth. And the worst part? He probably believed his own act. But it didn't matter because she finally saw what was real. The divine doesn't lie. Not forever. Sometimes, the forest waits and watches. And then, one evening, the curtain falls.

That was divine timing—not a lightning bolt or a public betrayal, but a gentle, irreversible unveiling.

Varsha no longer needed him to understand what he had done. She only needed to remember what she now knew. He was not a mirror. He was a mask and always had been.

This is what people don't understand about emotional manipulation. It doesn't always scream. Sometimes, it jokes. It flirts. It quotes Rumi. And when you finally recoil, it says, 'What? I was just being free.'

But freedom that disregards another's comfort is not freedom. It is entitlement. And now Varsha saw it for what it was.

THE POWER OF DIVINE TIMING

Varsha often asked herself why she hadn't seen it sooner—the subtle undermining, the shifting goalposts, the erosion of her confidence. The truth is, she couldn't have. Not back then. Her body had registered things her mind wasn't yet ready to accept. Sometimes we aren't strong enough to face the full truth of a person until we've built the inner scaffolding to hold it without collapsing.

This is where Divine Timing comes in. We like to believe clarity arrives through logic or effort, but in reality, it arrives through grace. The universe protects us from knowing certain things too early—not because we're weak, but because some truths are timed like ripening fruit. They fall when we're ready. Not a minute late, not a second too soon.

When Varsha finally saw Adesh clearly, it wasn't because the signs had suddenly appeared. It was because she had grown into someone who could finally *see*. This is the quiet mercy of Divine Timing: it doesn't ask us to rush. It simply waits until we are ready.

Control vs Divine Timing

What is divine timing? It is relinquishing control over how and when events should happen. Instead, we trust that whatever happens and whenever it happens is for our highest good.

We like to believe we're in control: That if we plan meticulously, make the right choices, and put in enough effort, our relationships will unfold exactly as we want them to. We set timelines, expectations, and milestones, assuming that love or friendship—like a project—will follow a structured path. But relationships don't work that way.

Some of the most profound connections in life happen when we least expect them. And some of the most painful separations occur despite our best efforts to hold on. Love has its own rhythm, and often, the more we try to force it, the more it resists. What if delays, obstacles, and heartbreaks are not rejections but redirections?

Being in tune with a relationship means understanding divine timing: why things don't always happen when we want them to, how to recognise when we're resisting the flow, and why trusting the process is often the most powerful thing we can do. Whether you're waiting for love, healing from loss, or struggling with the uncertainty of 'what comes next', this is an invitation to look beyond the immediate and trust that the universe knows what it's doing.

The Three Dimensions of Divine Timing in Love

1. Readiness: You Meet People When You Are Ready for Them

We often think that meeting the 'right person' at the 'right time' is purely about external circumstances—geography, career stage, or life events. But the deeper truth is that timing is largely internal. You meet people when you are emotionally, mentally, and spiritually ready for them.

Think about it: Have you ever met someone amazing but weren't in the right space to appreciate them? Or been deeply drawn to someone who wasn't ready for you? Readiness isn't about desire—it's about capacity. You may want love, but are you emotionally available? You may crave deep friendships, but are you capable of vulnerability?

This applies not only to romance but to all relationships. Sometimes, a mentor appears when you've reached a stage where you can absorb their wisdom. A friendship deepens when you're open to connection. And love, no matter how strong, struggles when one or both people are unprepared.

Key takeaway: People enter your life when you are ready for them—sometimes not a moment sooner. If something isn't happening, instead of asking, 'Why not yet?', ask, 'What within me still needs to grow?'

2. Alignment: The Right People Arrive When Paths Are Meant to Cross

Even if two people are 'ready', their connection depends on alignment—being in the right place, mentally and circumstantially, to build something together.

Many of us have met someone we connected with deeply, yet external circumstances pulled us apart. Maybe you met the perfect partner, but they were living abroad. Maybe a friendship faded because life took you in different directions. Maybe a mentor appeared years after you needed them.

Alignment is about synchronicity—not just being ready but being on converging paths. It's why you don't meet your best friend at five, your mentor at fifteen, or your soulmate at eighteen. Your lives have to align for the relationship to flourish.

This is why some people reunite years later when the timing is right. And why some relationships, despite deep love, fall apart due to misaligned priorities. It's not about love failing. It's about life moving differently.

Key takeaway: Not every love is meant to be acted on when you first feel it. Sometimes, timing is off because both people need to walk separate paths before coming together. And sometimes, those paths never cross again—that, too, is divine timing.

3. Cycles: Every Relationship Has Its Own Rhythm

We assume relationships follow a linear path: Meet, connect, grow, deepen, and last forever. In truth, relationships unfold in cycles—some short, some long, some repeating.

Many relationships include periods of separation and reunion—friendships that revive after years, exes who return changed, mentors who reappear in later life. Sometimes, space is needed to grow apart before reconnecting in a healthier way.

But cycles also mean some relationships are only for a season. Not every bond is meant to last a lifetime. Some teach us, support us through a phase, and dissolve when their purpose is complete. Forcing a temporary connection into permanence creates pain.

This is where trust in divine timing matters most—knowing when to hold on, when to let go, and when to allow life to bring someone back if it's meant to be.

Key takeaway: Every relationship follows its own rhythm. Some people leave, some return, and some stay. Trust the cycle instead of resisting it.

The Wisdom of Letting Go and Trusting Timing

If there's one truth about relationships, it's this: You cannot force timing. No matter how much you want a relationship to work, if the readiness, alignment, or cycle is off, it will feel like pushing against a closed door.

Trusting divine timing isn't passive—it doesn't mean waiting around and hoping things work out. It means doing the inner work, allowing life to unfold, and knowing that what is truly meant for you will never require you to chase it.

So, if a relationship isn't coming together the way you hoped, ask yourself:

- Am I truly ready for this connection?
- Are our lives aligned, or is something pulling us in different directions?
- Is this a cycle that's meant to continue, or has it served its purpose?

Sometimes, the hardest thing is accepting that not everything we love is meant to stay. But when we surrender to divine timing, we make space for something even greater than we imagined.

Relationships beyond Romance

When we talk about divine timing in love, it's easy to focus on romantic relationships—waiting for the right partner, navigating break-ups, or longing for a reunion. But divine timing isn't limited to romance. It applies to friendships, family bonds, mentorships, and even work relationships. Some people enter our lives at exactly the moment we need them, while others fade away despite our attempts to hold on. The same principles of divine timing apply across all these connections.

Love, in all its forms, operates on a rhythm we don't always understand. Some connections are immediate but fleeting, others take years to develop, and some feel right but happen at the wrong time. Why? Because relationships unfoldacross three dimensions of divine timing: Readiness, alignment, and cycles.

My friend met her mentor at 40, years after leaving her first career behind. She often wonders how different things would have been if they'd crossed paths earlier—but she knows now that she wasn't ready for that kind of guidance until she'd lived through her own lessons.

A Mythical Tale of Timing

Long before Damayanti met King Nala, she knew he was her destiny.

Even before they had seen each other, she had heard stories of his wisdom and kindness. She felt an unexplainable pull towards him, a knowing in her heart. They exchanged messages through a friendly swan who played Cupid in their story. Nala felt the same attraction towards Damayanti—he had dreamt of her before they met. It was as if their souls were already speaking.

But divine timing is rarely simple.

When Damayanti's *swayamvara* (a ceremony in which a woman chooses her husband from among a gathering of suitors) was announced, kings and princes from across the land arrived to win her hand. Among them were not only mortals but gods themselves. The gods—Indra, Varuna, Agni, and Yama—wished her to choose one of them. But Damayanti's heart already belonged to Nala.

The gods, testing her devotion, appeared at the swayamvara disguised as Nala. A line of identical Nalas stood before her, and she was told to choose. Yet Damayanti, calm in her trust, knew the real Nala from the gods. She noticed his feet touched the ground, he blinked, he was human—imperfect and real—and she chose him.

Her choice set their love story in motion, but divine timing had its own rhythm. Though they married in joy, Nala's fate took a dark turn. Cursed by Kali, he lost his kingdom and retreated into the forest. Burdened by guilt at the hardships Damayanti now faced, he abandoned her while she slept, believing she would be better off without him.

Damayanti awoke angry and hurt. Yet, her faith never wavered. She trusted their story was not over.

After enduring many hardships, she found her way back to her father's kingdom but did not despair. Instead, she rebuilt her life, becoming a strong and capable queen. Though she used her resources to track Nala, she did not seek him out—she felt it wasn't the right time. Only when she sensed that both had grown did she call for another swayamvara, knowing Nala would be ready. And so, life brought them together again. Nala returned not broken, but whole.

What makes Damayanti's story powerful isn't only her love—it's her unwavering trust in divine timing. She didn't chase Nala when he left. She didn't lose herself in waiting. She held to her faith that what was meant for her would return when the time was right.

And it did.

Their reunion wasn't the beginning of their love but the continuation of a journey that required them to walk separate paths before being together again.

Sometimes, divine timing asks us to trust when everything feels uncertain. Damayanti's patience was not passive; it was active faith. She lived fully, knowing love returns not through force, but through alignment.

Damayanti's maturity lay in recognising both her strengths and Nala's flaws yet still choosing to give their love another chance. Despite her grief, she acted with intelligence and resilience while trusting that destiny would reunite them when the time was right.

- She did not despair but took action. Disguised as a maid, she found work in a queen's court, proving her ability to survive independently rather than wallowing in suffering.

- She trusted in divine timing yet made efforts to find Nala. Trusting divine timing does not mean sitting idle; it means working on ourselves and having a plan. Damayanti sent messengers across kingdoms to seek news of him.
- She maintained patience without attachment. Though she longed for her husband, she did not lose herself in sorrow. She balanced longing with self-respect, embodying grace even in the waiting.
- She reunited with Nala when the time was right. Their reunion came only after he had gone through his own journey of growth and learnt from his mistakes.

Ancient stories understood well the concept of divine timing. Nala and Damayanti's tale is one of love written in the stars yet torn apart by fate. Their separation was not a punishment but a necessary journey of growth. When they finally reunited, it wasn't because Damayanti fought harder or Nala yielded more—it was because both had transformed.

The right love at the wrong time is still the wrong love.

Signs You Are Fighting Divine Timing

Many of us struggle with accepting the natural timing of relationships, believing that if we hold on, try harder, or push past obstacles, things will eventually fall into place. But divine timing doesn't work like that. It flows effortlessly when it should. When we resist it, the universe sends us signs—ones we often ignore.

Here are some unmistakable signs that you are fighting against divine timing in your relationships:

1. You Keep Forcing a Relationship That Isn't Flowing

A healthy relationship should feel like a natural exchange, not an uphill battle where you are the only one making an effort. If you are the one to constantly initiate conversations, make plans, or justify why this connection should work, it's a sign you're forcing something that isn't meant to be—at least not right now.

Ask yourself: *Am I the only one holding this together?* Healthy relationships have balance. If you are the only one fighting for it, it's time to stop resisting and allow the natural course of things to unfold.

2. You Are Holding on to Someone Who Has Moved On

One of the hardest truths to accept is when someone we love has emotionally, mentally, or physically moved on. Yet we cling to memories, signs, or the hope that they will 'realise' they still love us.

But if someone has repeatedly chosen a different path, that is a form of divine timing at work. People exit our lives for a reason, and holding on to them only blocks what is truly meant for us.

Ask yourself: *Am I waiting for someone who has stopped waiting for me?* If their actions show they have let go, it's time to honour that timing and free yourself.

3. You Feel Constant Resistance and Roadblocks

When something is meant for you, doors open effortlessly. But when you are out of sync with divine timing, you feel constant delays, miscommunications, obstacles, and emotional exhaustion.

Maybe every attempt at getting closer to someone results in misunderstanding. Maybe no matter how much effort you put in, external circumstances always pull you apart. These roadblocks aren't punishments—they are redirections.

Ask yourself: *Am I ignoring signs that this isn't working?* Sometimes, things don't come together because they're not meant to—at least not yet.

4. You Keep Romanticising 'What Could Have Been'

If you find yourself living in the past, replaying old memories, and fixating on how things *could* have been, you are resisting the present moment.

Yes, a relationship *could* have worked—if circumstances were different, if timing had been better, if one of you had made a different choice. But that's not what happened. Clinging to an alternate reality stops you from living in the one that exists now.

Ask yourself: *Am I more attached to the idea of this relationship than the reality of it?* If the only thing keeping you invested is nostalgia, it's time to release the past.

5. You Are Ignoring Your Growth

Sometimes, divine timing delays a relationship because *you* are not meant to be in that connection right now. Yet instead of focusing on personal growth, you stay stuck in waiting mode—putting your life on hold, obsessing over someone else's choices, and ignoring the lessons this period is trying to teach you.

Ask yourself: *Am I waiting for someone else to determine my happiness?* The right relationship will never require you to abandon your journey. If divine timing is making you wait, it's because something within you still needs to evolve.

6. You Are Holding on Because of Societal or Family Expectations

In many cultures, especially in India, the length of a relationship is often seen as proof of worthiness. The ability to 'keep people in your life' is glorified—whether it's childhood friendships, lifelong marriages, or decades-old family ties.

People proudly say, 'I've had the same best friend since we were five,' or 'We've been together since college.' And while that's beautiful, it also creates immense pressure. The underlying message is:

- You are a good friend only if your friendships last forever.
- You are successful in love only if you stay with one person your whole life.
- Letting go is a failure, not a natural part of life.

So, what happens when a relationship isn't working, but you feel guilty for letting it go?

You stay. Not because it's right for you, but because leaving makes you feel like you've failed.

Ask yourself: *Am I staying in this relationship because I truly want to, or because I feel obligated to prove something to my family or society?*

The truth is, letting go is not failure—it's wisdom. Not every relationship is meant to last a lifetime. Some people are meant to walk with you for a season, teach you something, and move on. Holding on just for the sake of longevity isn't love—it's fear of judgement.

True relationship success isn't about duration. It's about alignment. Are you still growing together, or are you just forcing an old connection because it feels safer than facing the unknown?

Surrendering to Divine Timing

When you stop fighting divine timing, you release anxiety and frustration. You stop chasing people who don't choose you. You stop forcing relationships that don't flow. And most importantly, you trust that what is truly meant for you will never pass you by.

Surrendering doesn't mean giving up—it means recognising that some things are meant to happen later, or not at all, and that this is a blessing in disguise.

If you see yourself in any of these signs, take a step back. Instead of fighting divine timing, start trusting it.

How to Let Go of the Timeline and Trust the Process

We often have a timeline in our minds: '*By this age, I should be married; by this year, I should have found my life partner; by now, this relationship should have worked out.*' But divine timing doesn't follow human deadlines. The more we force things to happen on our schedule, the more we struggle. Letting go of the timeline is about surrendering to the process while still showing up for life.

1. Shift from Control to Trust

Instead of thinking, '*Why hasn't this happened yet?*' shift to, '*What is this period teaching me?*' Trust that delays and detours are not punishments—they are protection and preparation.

2. Focus on the Present, Not the Outcome

Are you so focused on the future that you're missing what's

happening now? Instead of obsessing over whether a relationship will last forever, ask:

- Do I feel seen, valued, and respected today? (Remember, not everyone needs to see, value, and respect you. It is unrealistic to expect all and sundry to respect that you are unhealthy.)
- Am I growing as a person through this connection?

The right relationship will unfold naturally without constant anxiety about the future.

3. Recognise That Rejection Is Redirection

Not everything lost is a loss. Some doors close because they are not meant for you, even if you wanted them badly. A break-up, an unanswered message, or a fading friendship might be clearing space for something better.

4. Stop Comparing Your Journey

Your best friend got engaged, your cousin had an arranged marriage at 25, and your colleague is celebrating a tenth anniversary. So what? Their timeline is not yours. Your path is unfolding exactly as it's meant to.

5. Keep Moving Forward

Trusting divine timing doesn't mean sitting back and waiting for life to happen. Show up. Try. Love. Learn. But let go of the need to control *when* things should fall into place.

All these are easier said than done. It takes repeated reminders to stay aware and to practise trusting the universe and divine timing. When you trust the process, you stop chasing and start attracting. Life moves in ways you never expected—often delivering what you need, at exactly the right time. The universe is always working on your behalf, even in the pauses. Trust the pause.

10

Attachment Styles in Healing: Anxious, Secure, and Avoidant

Lily met Runa during their final year of university, on a winter evening thick with the scent of impending rain. They had both reached for the same worn-out copy of *The Bell Jar* at a campus book sale. Their fingers brushed, and they laughed. That was it. From that moment on, something sparked between them—a feeling of having found someone who *understood*.

It started simply. Study sessions in the library. Late-night walks to the tea stall by the lake. Sharing secrets in whispers, trading stories like treasures. Runa was magnetic—the kind of person who made everything feel a little more alive. Lily was drawn in immediately. She loved the way Runa made ordinary things feel sacred—a shared playlist, a handwritten letter, the silence that stretched comfortably between them on long afternoons.

At first, it was easy. They were inseparable. Friends often joked that they were like two halves of the same soul. Lily liked the idea of being so completely known by someone.

But slowly, something inside her started to shift.

When Runa didn't reply to her messages right away, Lily felt a tightness in her chest. She reasoned it was nothing; people get busy. But she'd find herself staring at her phone, waiting, checking if Runa had been online. She wondered if Runa was talking to someone else instead. She told herself it was normal to miss your closest friend this much. And yet, the longing felt sharper than it should have.

When Runa cancelled plans—because of a headache or because of a deadline—Lily's mind spun. *Was she pulling away? Had Lily said something wrong? Was Runa tired of her?* She'd scroll through their old conversations, searching for the exact moment things had started to change.

She didn't tell Runa how much time she spent thinking about their friendship. How she sometimes rehearsed their conversations in her head before they met just to make sure she didn't say something 'needy'. How she kept track of who texted first, and how long it took Runa to reply; and how relieved she felt when Runa sent a meme in the middle of the day, like nothing had changed at all. But it was exhausting.

One evening, they were sitting in Runa's tiny flat, listening to music, the window cracked open to let in the cool breeze. Runa was scrolling through something on her phone, and Lily was just watching her. Waiting. For what, she wasn't sure. And out of nowhere, Runa looked up and said, 'You feel . . . distant lately. Or maybe tense. Is something wrong?'

Lily almost laughed. *She* was distant? She wanted to tell Runa she was doing everything she could to stay close. She wanted to scream, *I'm trying so hard.* Instead, she shook her head. 'No, nothing's wrong,' she lied.

But that night, lying awake in her own bed, she admitted to herself that something *was* wrong. Not with Runa. With her. With how she was holding this friendship like it might shatter if she loosened her grip even slightly. She remembered doing this before—waiting by the door as a kid for her mother to come home from work, convinced that if she didn't wait, something bad would happen. Holding tightly to people who drifted away anyway.

A week later, she booked a session with a therapist. She wasn't sure what to say at first, but it tumbled out eventually—the friendship, the anxiety, the fear that she was too much and not enough, all at once. Her therapist listened and nodded, then asked gently, 'What happens if you let Runa come closer on her own terms? What happens if you stop holding on so tightly?'

Lily didn't know. The thought terrified her. But slowly, she began to try. She didn't message Runa every time she thought of her. She made plans with other people. She let herself sit in the discomfort of not knowing where she stood every single moment.

This was a slow process of unlearning and relearning, but something surprising happened. The friendship didn't fall apart. In fact, it grew steadier. Without the pressure, their conversations felt lighter. Runa reached out more. Lily stopped bracing for the moment she would leave.

One afternoon, sitting by the lake again, Runa said, 'I like you like this, you know. Like you're here because you *want* to be. Not because you're afraid not to be.'

Lily smiled. It had taken her time to understand that. That real connection doesn't have to be held tightly. That love—even friendship-love—needs room to breathe.

She still loved Runa deeply. But now, she loved herself, too. And that made all the difference.

ATTACHMENT AND EARLY RELATIONAL PATTERNS

In every interaction with another, we connect, seek comfort, or withdraw. Over time, these interactions form patterns that get deeply embedded in our subconscious. They shape the way we love, trust, and experience relationships.

Like most psychological traits, our attachment style is rooted in childhood. Our earliest bonds, particularly with our primary caregivers, set the foundation for how we relate to closeness, security, and emotional intimacy. If we grow up watching a parent withdraw from uncomfortable emotions, dismiss our feelings, or respond inconsistently to our needs, we internalise these patterns. Sometimes we mirror them directly, and other times we develop contrasting responses. Either way, what we experience shapes our default settings in relationships.

The impact of parental attunement—whether it is emotional closeness, inconsistency, or neglect—leaves an imprint on the subconscious mind. If our emotions were often overlooked in favour of task completion or external success, we may grow up prioritising achievement over emotional expression. If, on the other hand, we were raised in an environment that nurtured feelings and emphasised emotional closeness, we are more likely to seek and create relationships that reflect that warmth and security.

Attachment patterns do not form overnight. They are reinforced through adolescence and adulthood, each time we respond to another person's friendship, closeness, or distance. When faced with emotional intimacy, do we lean in, or do we instinctively step back? Do we seek reassurance in relationships, or do we withdraw to avoid vulnerability?

Transactional Love and Attachment

Parental neglect doesn't always appear as outright abandonment; sometimes, it takes the form of conditional affection. If love and validation were given only in exchange for achievements—being a 'good child' to receive praise, scoring high marks to earn a reward—children internalise the belief that love must be earned. This often manifests in adulthood as a tendency to over-give, people-please, or perform to meet others' expectations to feel worthy of love.

Conversely, individuals raised in environments where emotions were dismissed as unnecessary or excessive may suppress their own needs and avoid deep emotional connections altogether.

The Nervous System's Role in Attachment

Beyond psychology and behaviour, attachment patterns are deeply connected to the nervous system. Early relational experiences shape how our body perceives safety or threat in emotional situations. If a child grows up with caregivers who provide consistent comfort and emotional regulation, their nervous system learns to associate closeness with safety. They are more likely to feel secure in relationships, trusting others and managing emotions with the attention they deserve.

However, if a child experiences unpredictability, neglect, or emotional dismissal, their nervous system remains in a heightened state of alertness, constantly scanning for potential rejection or pain. This can lead to overreacting to perceived threats (becoming anxious and hyper-vigilant) or shutting down and withdrawing (becoming avoidant). The nervous system doesn't just influence how we feel in relationships—it shapes our core survival responses to connection itself.

Cultural Influences on Attachment

While attachment patterns have biological and psychological roots, they are also shaped by culture. Societies differ in the way they promote relational styles. For example, Western cultures, which emphasise independence and individualism, often foster avoidant tendencies, where self-sufficiency is seen as a strength. In contrast, collectivist cultures, which prioritise family and interdependence, may encourage closer emotional bonds but can also reinforce anxious attachment due to strong social expectations around relationships.

Additionally, cultural norms dictate how emotions are expressed. In some cultures, open expression is encouraged. Not only is free expression encouraged, but the individual is supported sans judgement. This exchange reinforces emotional safety. In other cultures, restraint is valued, teaching individuals to suppress their needs or manage them privately rather than express them. These cultural differences influence not just how we attach but also how we perceive and interpret emotional closeness and distance.

THREE ATTACHMENT STYLES

In relationships, how we connect, communicate, and handle emotions often traces back to our attachment style. Attachment is the underlying blueprint that shapes how we seek closeness, manage conflict, and respond to emotional needs—our own and others'. While these patterns are rooted in early childhood experiences, they continue to influence our relationships throughout life.

Broadly, attachment styles fall into three primary categories: Secure, anxious, and avoidant. However, attachment is not always rigid. Many individuals exhibit traits from more than one style, shifting based on context and personal growth.

1. Secure Attachment: Trust and Emotional Availability

People with a secure attachment style are comfortable with both emotional closeness and independence. They trust others, communicate openly, and manage conflict without feeling threatened. They don't fear abandonment, nor do they feel suffocated by intimacy. This balance allows them to form relationships based on mutual respect rather than fear or dependency.

Mithun and Eesha have been dating for three years. When Eesha starts a new job in another city, Mithun is supportive. He reassures her of their strong bond and trusts that they will maintain their connection. They discuss their concerns openly and make a plan to stay emotionally close despite the distance. Their ability to communicate and trust each other keeps their relationship stable.

2. Anxious Attachment: Seeking Reassurance and Fear of Abandonment

Those with an anxious attachment style deeply crave closeness but often fear being abandoned. Their emotions tend to be intense, and they may seek constant reassurance in relationships. When they perceive distance or lack of responsiveness, they can become preoccupied with doubts, often over-analysing their partner's actions or words.

Akshata and her best friend, Neha, have been inseparable for years. When Neha starts spending more time with a new group of friends, Akshata feels insecure. She begins calling Neha repeatedly, fearing she is being replaced. When Neha doesn't immediately reply, Akshata assumes the worst and spirals into self-doubt. Her anxious attachment makes her sensitive to any perceived emotional distance.

3. Avoidant Attachment: Fear of Intimacy and Need for Independence

Avoidant attachment is marked by discomfort with emotional closeness. Individuals with this style value independence and often withdraw when they sense emotional intensity. They may struggle to express their feelings and find it difficult to rely on others, fearing that too much closeness will make them feel trapped.

Vikram grew up in a household where emotions were rarely discussed. Now, as an adult, he finds it difficult to express affection. His sister, Priya, often tries to talk to him about family matters, but he keeps conversations surface-level and avoids discussing feelings. When Priya expresses frustration over his emotional distance, Vikram brushes it off, feeling uncomfortable with deep emotional engagement.

The Anxious-Avoidant Trap: Why These Two Styles Attract

It is common for people with anxious and avoidant attachment styles to be drawn to each other. The anxious person seeks closeness and reassurance, while the avoidant person pulls away from emotional intensity. This creates a cycle where the anxious partner feels neglected and chases validation, while the avoidant partner feels overwhelmed and withdraws further.

At first, the attraction may be strong—the anxious partner admires the avoidant's independence, while the avoidant partner enjoys the warmth and affection of the anxiously attached person. But over time, their core fears are reinforced in their relationship. The more the anxious person demands closeness, the more the avoidant person feels smothered and distances themselves. Unless both partners recognise this pattern and work to create balance, the relationship can become a cycle of pursuit and withdrawal.

Attachment as a Spectrum: Blending Styles and Growth

Attachment is not always clear-cut. Many people exhibit traits from more than one style, depending on the situation. A person might feel secure in friendships but anxious in romantic relationships. Others may shift from avoidant to secure attachment over time as they build trust and self-awareness.

Understanding attachment styles is not about labelling oneself or others, but about recognising patterns. The more we become aware of these dynamics, the better we can work towards secure, fulfilling relationships—whether in romance, friendships, or family.

Laila's Avoidance, Majnu's Anxiousness

The ancient tragic love story of Laila and Majnu offers a striking depiction of anxious and avoidant attachment dynamics.

In the desert lands of Rajasthan, where sands whisper secrets of love and longing, lived a boy named Qays. He was born into wealth, but none of it mattered the day he saw Laila. She was dark-eyed, sharp-witted, carrying an air of untouchable grace. From the moment their eyes met, Qays became Majnu—the mad one, lost in a love he could neither possess nor abandon.

Laila felt the pull, too, but she was careful. In her world, love was duty and obedience. As Majnu's devotion deepened, so did his madness. His poetry filled the desert winds, his longing etched into every word. People marvelled, pitied, and scorned him, but he didn't care. For Majnu, Laila was truth, prayer, existence. Yet each time he reached for her, she retreated, bound by family honour.

Her father, angered by Majnu's obsession, locked her away and married her off to another. Majnu couldn't accept this. He wandered the deserts, spoke to wild animals, and carved Laila's name on temple stones. He abandoned the world, convinced that if he loved her enough—or suffered enough—she would be his.

But Laila was bound by duty, caught in obligations she couldn't escape.

Majnu lived in exile, consumed by longing, until news of Laila's death reached him. He collapsed in the desert, a faint smile on his lips, believing he would finally be reunited with her.

Their story became legend: A love so mad it destroyed them both. But was it genuinely love? Or something desperate, something patterned long before they met?

Majnu loved like a drowning man, clinging to survival. Laila built walls, protecting herself from his flood. The world calls it a tragedy. Perhaps it is a lesson—hidden in the sands of time.

Majnu's attachment style leaned heavily towards anxious preoccupation, leading him to persist in his pursuit of Laila even when circumstances made their union impossible. Like many anxiously attached individuals, he became consumed by his emotions, disregarding external realities and the level of commitment reciprocated by Laila. People with an anxious attachment style often place their partners on a pedestal, seeking validation and reassurance at the cost of their well-being. When love becomes the sole source of meaning, the loss or absence of that love turns into unbearable suffering.

Laila, in contrast, displayed avoidant tendencies. Whether or not she loved Majnu with the same intensity is unclear, but she was able to regulate her emotions better and didn't mirror Majnu's desperation. Classic avoidant patterns include maintaining emotional distance, resisting deep vulnerability, or prioritising duty over personal feelings. In Laila's case, external pressures—family obligations and societal expectations—played a significant role in her decision-making. However, despite her emotional restraint, she was aware of the impact she had on Majnu. Avoidantly attached individuals often struggle with fully engaging in intense emotional experiences, fearing the loss of control or the weight of deep emotional entanglement.

Had both Laila and Majnu possessed secure attachment styles, their story might have unfolded differently. Securely attached individuals communicate their needs and emotions clearly, fostering mutual understanding rather than imbalance. They would have openly discussed the societal barriers they faced, weighing the consequences of pursuing their love. If separation were inevitable, they would have communicated their feelings with respect, offering each other closure rather than unresolved longing. Their healing would then have become a personal journey of growth, rather than one marked by devastation and obsession.

HOW TO IDENTIFY YOUR ATTACHMENT STYLE

Every relationship you've been in—romantic, familial, or platonic—carries clues about your attachment style. The way you respond to closeness, handle emotional needs, and navigate conflict reveals the patterns you follow. Identifying your style is not about locking yourself in a rigid category. It's about recognising tendencies so you can improve the way you connect with others.

Review Your Past Relationships

One of the simplest ways to identify your attachment style is to reflect on your emotions and behaviour in relationships. Ask yourself:

- ➢ Do I feel anxious when someone I care about becomes distant?

- Do I feel overwhelmed when someone tries to get too close too quickly?
- Do I generally feel secure, trusting that conflict or space doesn't mean abandonment?

Anxious attachment often shows up as seeking reassurance, overextending, or fearing abandonment. Avoidant attachment leans towards pulling away, minimising emotions, or feeling suffocated by closeness. Secure attachment balances closeness and independence, trusting that relationships can weather ups and downs.

Emotional Needs, Conflict, and Self-Sabotage

Your reactions in daily life offer more clues:

- Do you try to 'earn' love through over-giving? (Anxious)
- Do you view emotional dependence as weakness? (Avoidant)
- Are you comfortable expressing needs without fear? (Secure)

In conflict, anxious types may panic or rush to fix, while avoidants withdraw. Secure individuals can stay engaged without spiralling. Self-sabotage also follows these patterns: The anxious chase unavailable partners, avoidants push away those who care, and secure individuals feel safe to remain open.

Different Styles in Different Relationships

Attachment isn't fixed. You may show one style at work, another in friendships, and yet another in romance.

Kapila, for instance, is a successful entrepreneur with an avoidant style at work—professional, detached, focused on efficiency. At home, however, she is anxiously attached to her husband, overextending to keep the relationship intact. With friends, she again leans avoidant, preferring to cut ties rather than address conflict. Like many of us, she shifts unconsciously across contexts.

Attachment doesn't only shape romance. It colours friendships, family ties, workplace dynamics, and how we relate to ourselves.

Context	Anxious Type	Avoidant Type	Secure Type
Friendships	Worry about being liked	Keep a tight circle and resist emotional demands	Trust that space doesn't mean disinterest
Family	Early caregiver bonds influence connection or insecurity	Carry tension and avoidance into adulthood	Develop healthier bonds with balance and trust
Workplace	Seek approval	Prefer independence	Balance feedback, teamwork, and leadership
Romantic Relationships	Seek closeness	Prioritise independence	Maintain a healthy balance between closeness and autonomy
Spirituality and Self	Engage in self-critical inner dialogue	Avoid reflection	Trust in growth and embrace self-development

Can Attachment Styles Change?

Yes. These patterns are learnt, not hardwired. Anxious individuals can grow confident, avoidants can learn intimacy, and anyone can move towards security through:

- Therapy: Uncovering root wounds and practising new patterns.
- Life experiences: Supportive partners, friendships, or even difficult break-ups.
- Self-work: Emotional regulation, boundaries, and self-trust.

This process is often called earned secure attachment—gaining balance through intentional growth.

Tools for Developing Security

Some effective tools include:

- Therapy for insight and guidance
- Mindfulness to separate past fears from present experience
- Self-soothing to regulate emotions without constant reassurance
- Healthy boundaries to balance openness with self-respect

Secure relationships also serve as models. Being around people who communicate clearly and provide emotional safety helps anxious types feel stable and avoidants become more comfortable with closeness.

Healing through Self-Awareness

Simply knowing your attachment style is a powerful start. But awareness must be paired with practice. When you notice yourself reacting anxiously or avoidantly, pause and ask:

- Is this reaction rooted in the past or the present?
- What need am I trying to meet—security, control, or self-protection?
- How can I respond in a way that reflects the kind of relationships I want?

Even two insecurely attached people can build a healthy relationship if both commit to growth. Without awareness, though, the cycle of anxiety and avoidance continues.

No Attachment Style Is 'Bad'

There is no wrong style—only patterns that either support or hinder connection. The goal isn't to erase your history but to move forward with awareness. The more you understand your attachment tendencies, the more fulfilling, safe, and balanced your relationships can become.

11

Detaching with Grace: Vairagya and the Art of Non-Attachment

In Canadian writer Yann Martel's globally successful book, *Life of Pi*, there is a moment at the end that is quietly devastating and profoundly illuminating. After months of unimaginable struggle at sea, surviving hunger, fear, and despair, Pi Patel and the Bengal tiger, Richard Parker, finally wash ashore on the coast of Mexico. Pi is barely alive—his body broken, his spirit frayed—but in his heart, there remains one fragile hope. He believes that, after everything they have endured together, there will be a final acknowledgement. A glance back. A pause. Some small gesture that honours their shared journey. After all, they had both crossed the vast, indifferent ocean together, reliant on one another for survival. Surely, that counted for something.

But Richard Parker does not turn around. He steps off the lifeboat, silent and indifferent, and disappears into the jungle without so much as a backwards glance. No farewell. No acknowledgement. No closure.

Pi lies in the sand, devastated. The pain of abandonment strikes deeper than the wounds on his flesh. 'I wept like a child,' he later recalls, not from relief at having survived, but from the raw ache of an ending he never expected. After everything, how could Richard Parker leave?

That's the nature of life, isn't it? Relationships, experiences, and even suffering itself come into our lives, shape us in ways both beautiful and brutal, and then move on—often without warning or ceremony. We crave a proper goodbye. We want closure—an explanation, an apology, a gesture of gratitude, a sense of mutual recognition. And when we don't receive it, we often suffer more from the absence of that ending than from the experience itself.

Pi's heartbreak is deeply human. It speaks to something universal in all of us—the longing for resolution. We yearn for endings that are neat, respectful, and fair. But life rarely obliges. People walk away. Circumstances change abruptly. Conversations are left unfinished. Love stories dissolve without clarity. And what is left behind is an ache we struggle to name.

Vairagya can help in such—and all—life situations.

Vairagya, the practice of detachment, does not mean indifference. It does not demand that we harden our hearts or deny the depth of our feelings. Instead, it calls for a quiet acceptance of the impermanence woven into the fabric of life. True Vairagya is the wisdom to let go without bitterness, without clinging, without demanding that life tie up its loose ends with a tidy bow.

Richard Parker walking away from Pi wasn't a rejection of their shared past. It wasn't ingratitude. It was simply the tiger being true to his nature, answering his own call, stepping into the next phase of his journey with no drama and no goodbye. Just movement.

And so it is with many people and moments in our lives. Sometimes they exit quietly, without explanation and in ways that feel deeply unfair. But their leaving is not always a verdict on what was shared. It is simply life in motion.

When we hold on tightly—to relationships, old identities, the belief that things *should* have ended differently—we suffer. We trap ourselves in a story that has already moved on. But when we loosen our grip, when we release the expectation of closure, we free ourselves. We lighten our load for the road ahead.

Vairagya invites us to trust that what we need will stay, and what is meant to leave will leave, whether we are ready or not. It asks us to meet these moments not with resistance but with grace.

So, ask yourself: When your own Richard Parker moments come—when someone leaves without explanation, when life changes course without warning—will you run after them, begging for closure that may never come? Or will you take a deep breath, feel the earth beneath your feet, and step forward, carrying the lessons but leaving the weight behind?

Vairagya is not about forgetting. It's about remembering without pain. Loving without needing. Living without grasping.

Like Pi on the shore, you may weep. But in the attitude of Vairagya, when the tears dry, you will rise. And like Richard Parker, you, too, will walk forward, into the unknown, free.

WHAT IS DETACHMENT?

The word detachment gets a bad reputation. People hear it and immediately think of coldness, indifference, or a kind of emotionless void. If someone says, 'I'm detached,' it often comes across as 'I don't care', which is incorrect.

Detachment, or Vairagya, does not mean suppressing your feelings, nor is it about not being controlled by what you feel. It's about experiencing life fully, without being ruled by every emotional high and low. Think of it as standing in the middle of a storm but not resisting or fighting the force.

Let's bust some of the biggest myths about detachment.

Myth #1: Detachment Means Not Caring

In fact, true detachment allows you to care more freely and deeply—without fear, insecurity, or the constant need for validation. You understand that when it is time to let go, you *will* let go with the confidence that you will recover from the pain it causes. When you are attached to someone or something, your emotions become entangled in expectations: *Will they love me back? Will this work out? What if I lose this?* Such attachment creates anxiety, possessiveness, and suffering.

Detachment, on the other hand, lets you love without clinging. It's the difference between holding a bird so tightly that you crush it and allowing it to perch in your hand willingly. You still care. You still love. But you don't feel desperate to control the outcome.

Consider friendships: When you stop being needy or afraid of losing someone, the relationship flows more smoothly, right? That's what detachment does. It removes desperation, not love.

Myth #2: Vairagya Means Renouncing Everything

People often believe that to be detached, one must give up their job, relationships, and worldly pleasures—maybe even run off to a cave in the Himalayas. However, Vairagya is not about physical renunciation; it's about internal freedom.

You can live in a palace and still be detached. Equally, you can be a monk in a cave and still be deeply attached to your ego. True detachment doesn't depend on your location or possessions; it depends on how much power those things have over you.

Take King Janaka (Sita's father in the Ramayana), ruler of Mithila, for instance. He was a great ruler, wealthy and powerful, but he was also a realised soul. He ruled his kingdom with complete involvement, yet he wasn't emotionally shackled by it. When a fire broke out in his palace and people around him were running helter-skelter to save as many valuables as they could, King Janaka was calm and composed amid that chaos.

He understood that his identity and peace were not tied to material possessions. While others panicked over what they might lose, Janaka remained unshaken, knowing that everything in the physical world is temporary. His detachment wasn't about carelessness; it was about deep wisdom—the realisation that his true self was beyond wealth, loss, and even the impermanence of the material world. Whether the palace stood or turned to ashes, his inner state remained unaffected. That was the strength of his Vairagya. That's true detachment—being fully present in life without being enslaved by it.

Myth #3: Detachment Makes You Emotionless

Many people believe that detachment means becoming a robot. No joy, no sadness, no excitement—just a blank, Zen-like stare into the void. That's not detachment. That's emotional suppression, which is completely unhealthy.

Vairagya doesn't mean you don't feel emotions. It means you don't get stuck in them. You experience them, you acknowledge them, and then you let them pass. Think of emotions like waves in the ocean—they come, they go. You don't have to drown in them.

You can cry, you can laugh, you can grieve, you can celebrate—but you don't let these emotions define you. That's true detachment.

Emotional Detachment vs Spiritual Detachment

Now, let's clear up another common confusion. People often mix up emotional detachment with spiritual detachment—but they're not the same.

- Emotional detachment (which is often unhealthy) is when people cut themselves off from feelings to avoid getting hurt. It's when someone shuts down emotionally, avoids relationships, or refuses to engage deeply with life. This is more like numbness than detachment.
- Spiritual detachment (which is Vairagya) is when you are fully present in life but don't get attached to outcomes. You feel emotions, but they don't control you. You engage in relationships, but you don't try to possess people. You enjoy material things, but you don't let them define your happiness.

A person with emotional detachment might say, 'I don't care about love or relationships. It's all pointless.' A person with spiritual detachment would say, 'I love deeply, but I am not afraid of losing it. Love is an experience, not a possession.'

See the difference? One is running away. The other is embracing life without fear.

So, What Does True Detachment Look Like?

Imagine watching a sunset. You admire its beauty, feel the moment deeply, but you don't try to hold onto it. You don't cry when it fades. You don't chase after it, demanding that it stay in the sky. You let it go, knowing that another sunset will come tomorrow.

That's detachment. You engage, you experience, but don't cling.

Can we do the same? Can we live, love, experience, and then let go without demanding closure, without clinging, without making every moment about ownership?

That's the essence of Vairagya.

True detachment is about being fully present in life without fear, without clinging, and without letting your happiness depend on things that are constantly changing.

And once you master that? You'll find that life feels lighter, love feels freer, and joy comes naturally, because you're no longer holding on so tightly.

What Vairagya Is Not, and How to Tell the Difference

Vairagya, or true detachment, is often misunderstood. Many believe they're practising it when, in fact, they're avoiding emotions, suppressing feelings, or becoming indifferent. Here's how to tell the difference.

1. Detachment vs Avoidance

Avoidance looks like detachment but isn't. Imagine someone betrayed in love who declares, 'I'm done with relationships.' They haven't let go; they're running from the fear of being hurt again. That's avoidance, not Vairagya. True detachment means engaging fully with life, knowing nothing is permanent. You can love deeply and still be at peace if it ends. That's freedom—not escape, but acceptance.

2. Detachment vs Indifference

Some mistake indifference for detachment. For instance, a father avoids showing love, claiming, 'Feelings make you weak.' Over time, he grows distant and isolated. That's emotional withdrawal, not Vairagya. True Vairagya isn't about not caring. It's about caring without clinging. You love, give, and engage—without losing your inner balance.

3. Detachment vs Emotional Suppression

Detachment isn't the absence of emotion but the freedom not to be ruled by it. Take someone who loses a job and says, 'I don't care,' while burying fear and shame inside. That's suppression, not detachment.

Real Vairagya means feeling the pain, processing it, and moving on lightly. 'This hurts, but it doesn't define me,' is the voice of true detachment.

4. The Litmus Test: Are You Free?

Ask yourself:

- Am I avoiding pain? → That's avoidance
- Have I stopped caring? → That's indifference
- Am I numbing my feelings? → That's suppression
- Do I feel light and free, no matter what happens? → That's Vairagya

Real detachment isn't closing your heart to life. It's living fully, knowing nothing truly belongs to you. It's inner freedom—not escape, but deeper engagement.

THE ESSENCE OF VAIRAGYA

Vairagya isn't about walking away from life; it's about walking *through* life with lightness. It's not about disconnecting from people but about loving without clinging. It's not about suppressing feelings but about not being ruled by them.

Think of a river flowing to the ocean. It meets obstacles, bends around them, but never stops moving. That's Vairagya—flowing with life instead of resisting it. The more you practise it, the more you realise that true freedom isn't in holding on—it's in knowing you're complete, whether something stays or goes.

Madhavi: The Woman Who Let Go

Princess Madhavi was born into royalty, the daughter of King Yayati and Queen Devayani of the Chandravanshi dynasty. Her life, however, was not destined for comfort or romance. Instead, she was called to a path of profound detachment—Vairagya.

Her father, Yayati, was a man enslaved by desire. Even after being cursed with old age by Sage Shukracharya for his endless indulgences, Yayati found a way to continue his pursuit of pleasure. His youngest son, Puru, took his father's curse upon himself, allowing Yayati to enjoy youth for a thousand more years. But endless enjoyment brought no lasting satisfaction. Eventually, Yayati realised that no amount of pleasure could fill his emptiness. His attachment to youth and desire only deepened his suffering.

Madhavi, however, lived differently. Her life became a lesson in letting go.

Sage Galava, Yayati's court sage, had pledged an impossible gurudakshina to his teacher, Vishwamitra: Eight hundred white horses with black ears. Desperate, Galava turned to King Yayati for help. The king had no such horses but offered something else—his daughter, Madhavi.

Madhavi was blessed with two extraordinary gifts: The power to bear strong sons to kings and the ability to regain her virginity after childbirth. Yayati proposed that Galava offer Madhavi to the powerful kings in exchange for the rare horses.

Galava, bound by his promise, agreed. Madhavi's consent was neither sought nor given. She became a bargaining tool, a way to settle a debt.

Her journey began with King Haryashva of Ayodhya. In return for two hundred horses, Madhavi bore him a son, Vasu. When her role was fulfilled, she quietly left. Next was King Divodasa of Kashi, for another two hundred horses. She bore him Pratardana and moved on. Then came King Ushinara of Bhoja, with whom she had Shibi. Finally, she bore Vrihadratha to King Bharata.

Each time, Madhavi surrendered to her fate, giving life and walking away. She was neither bitter nor resentful. She did not hold on to her sons or long to be kept as a queen. Kings who wanted to possess her found they could not. Madhavi accepted her path with grace. Her heart remained unattached, her spirit untouched.

Unlike her father, who clung desperately to youth and pleasure, Madhavi let go at every turn. She was passed from one kingdom to another, yet she carried no burden of regret. She did what was asked of her, and then she moved forward, free of longing.

When Galava finally returned to Vishwamitra, he had gathered only six hundred horses, far short of the original promise. Yet he brought Madhavi's four sons—powerful heirs to great kingdoms. Vishwamitra, recognising the effort and devotion behind the offering, accepted it. Galava's debt was repaid.

Madhavi, however, did not return to her father's palace. Nor did she stay with any of her sons. When her duty was done, she chose to leave it all behind. She retreated into the forest, embracing the solitary life of an ascetic. She renounced the world of power, kingship, and attachments. She chose freedom.

The Contrast Between Yayati and Madhavi

Yayati's life was a lesson in the suffering caused by attachment. Even after a thousand years of youth, he found no peace. Madhavi, on the other hand, lived by the essence of Vairagya—not by choice at first, but by circumstance. In time, she embodied it fully. She let go without bitterness, without clinging. While Yayati fought against time and loss, Madhavi surrendered and transcended.

Her story speaks to us today. How often do we cling to relationships, ambitions, or identities that no longer serve us? How often do we resist change, afraid to lose what we have? Madhavi teaches that true detachment is not rejection of life but freedom from its grip. It's the strength to walk away without resentment and to give without expecting anything in return.

Madhavi is rarely mentioned in grand tales, yet her life holds one of the most profound lessons of all. She showed that Vairagya is not coldness, nor is it resignation. It is power—the power to let go and still remain whole.

In the end, Madhavi owned nothing. But more importantly, nothing owned her.

The Role of Love in Vairagya

One of the biggest misconceptions about detachment is that it means a lack of love. People assume that if you are truly detached, you don't care, you don't feel, and you don't form deep bonds. But Vairagya isn't the opposite of love—it's the highest form of it.

Think about parents who raise their children with unconditional love but don't try to control their lives. They guide, support, and nurture them, but they don't cling. When the time comes for their children to leave home, they let them go with grace, knowing their love isn't diminished by distance. That is Vairagya in action.

Love without detachment is often filled with fear—fear of loss, fear of change, fear of not being loved back. But love with detachment is free, expansive, and fearless. It allows you to love fully without suffocating the other person.

A real-life example? Think of someone who holds on too tightly in a relationship. They check their partner's messages, need constant reassurance, and panic at the thought of separation. This isn't love—it's attachment, and attachment breeds insecurity. On the other hand, a person who practises Vairagya can love deeply, but if the relationship ends, they don't fall apart. They grieve, but they don't become lost.

True detachment doesn't take away love—it makes it purer. It's loving someone, not because you need them, but because you choose to, without fear, without possession, and without expectations.

How to Practice Vairagya Daily?

Most people assume Vairagya is for monks sitting in caves or sages meditating in forests. However, true detachment isn't about running away from life—it's about fully living it without being enslaved by it. You don't have to renounce the world to practice Vairagya. You just need to shift the way you engage with it.

So, how do you bring detachment into your everyday life?

1. Mindset Shifts: Seeing the World as It Is

Vairagya starts in the mind. Before you can practise it, you need to change the way you see the world.

a. **Understand impermanence:** Everything you hold dear—your relationships, your job, your body—is temporary. This isn't meant to be depressing; it's freeing. When you truly accept that nothing lasts forever, you stop clinging. You stop fearing loss because you understand that change is inevitable.

   A simple exercise: Think about something you worried about five years ago. Maybe it was a job interview, a break-up, or a financial struggle. It felt like the end of the world then. But today? You've moved on. The intensity of that moment faded. Realising this helps you let go of anxieties in the present.

b. **Observe without attachment:** We get tangled in emotions because we identify with them. But what if you could step back and just watch?

   Try this: The next time you feel overwhelmed—angry at a colleague, hurt by a friend, frustrated in traffic—pause. Instead of reacting, observe. Tell yourself, *I am feeling anger right now. I am feeling disappointed.* The moment you do this, you create space between yourself and the emotion. You are no longer angry; you are simply aware of it. That space is detachment.

2. Practical Exercises to Cultivate Detachment

Detachment isn't just a mindset—it's a practice. And like any skill, the more you work at it, the easier it becomes.

a. **Journalling to get thoughts out of your head:** One of the biggest traps of attachment is overthinking. We replay conversations, obsess over what people think, and get stuck in mental loops. Journalling is a great way to break this cycle.

At the end of each day, write down: One thing you got too attached to (a negative comment, an expectation, an outcome), how it made you feel, and what you can do to let it go.

Over time, you'll start seeing patterns. And when you see patterns, you can change them.

b. **Meditate to let go in real time:** Vipassana meditation, one of the oldest forms of mindfulness, is built around the idea of non-attachment. It teaches you to observe bodily sensations and emotions without reacting to them.

Start small. Sit for five minutes. Close your eyes. Focus on your breath. Thoughts will come—about work, about your to-do list, about that awkward conversation with your boss. Instead of engaging with them, just watch them float by like clouds. The more you practise this, the more you learn to detach from thoughts in daily life.

c. **Chanting mantras to train the mind to release attachments:** Repetition is a powerful tool for rewiring the brain. Mantras like *Om Mani Padme Hum* (Buddhist tradition) or *Aham Brahmasmi* (Vedantic tradition) are designed to anchor the mind, creating inner steadiness. Even repeating a simple phrase like *Let go* or *This, too, shall pass* can shift your emotional state.

3. Applying Vairagya in Daily Life

Now comes the real test—practising detachment where it matters.

a. **In relationships (love without clinging):** Many people think detachment means not forming close relationships. The truth? Detachment allows you to love better because you love without fear.

   Imagine you're in a relationship, and your partner is suddenly distant. The attached mind panics: *Why are they pulling away? What did I do wrong?* But the detached mind understands: *They are going through something. I cannot control them, only support them.*

   Detachment doesn't mean you stop caring; it means you stop controlling. It allows you to show up with love, without being consumed by expectations.

b. **At work (doing your best without over-identification):** Many people tie their self-worth to their jobs. If their project fails, they feel like a failure. If their boss criticises them, they take it personally.

   Detachment at work means giving your best effort but not attaching your entire identity to success or failure. A great example? A CEO who builds a company with passion but is ready to walk away if it no longer aligns with their future. They work hard, but they don't *cling*. That's detachment in action.

c. **Handling disappointments (letting go of outcomes):** Say you poured your heart into something—a job application, a business deal, a relationship—and it didn't work out. The attached mind spirals: *This shouldn't have happened! It's unfair!* The detached mind acknowledges, *I tried my best. It didn't work out. What's next?*

   A simple practice? When something doesn't go your way, instead of asking, '*Why is this happening to me?*' say, '*What is this teaching me?*' This shift alone can change your life.

4. Modern-Day Examples of Vairagya

a. **Buddhist monks (letting go of the ego):** Many Buddhist monks practice a ritual where they create intricate mandalas out of sand only to destroy them immediately after. It's a lesson in non-attachment: Nothing is permanent, and clinging is pointless.

b. **Artists who detach from their work:** Famous writer Elizabeth Gilbert (*Eat, Pray, Love*) talks about treating creativity with detachment. Instead of obsessing over whether a book will be a success or failure, she just writes. She releases the outcome. And ironically, that's when the best work happens.

c. **Someone leaving a toxic relationship gracefully:** Imagine one in a long-term relationship where she isn't valued. The attached person stays, hoping things will change. The detached person recognises: 'I love this person, but I cannot force them to love me back.' They walk away with grace, knowing their worth isn't tied to someone else's treatment of them. That is Vairagya.

Living with Lightness

Detachment isn't about becoming emotionless; it's about becoming emotionally free. It's about walking through life without being weighed down by every passing storm. When you practise Vairagya daily through mindset shifts, meditation, and conscious choices, you move from fear to peace, from clinging to flow.

And the best part? The lighter you walk through life, the more beautiful it becomes.

12

Rituals for Release: Letting-Go Ceremonies

I share the story below with care and the utmost respect—for my ancestors, for the mystery of spiritual work, and for the long arc of healing I continue to walk. It is not an easy story to tell. But it stands as one of the most powerful lessons I've ever received in what it truly means to let go—especially when we don't have the full picture, or even the words, to explain what we're releasing.

Swords and Roses

In the searing summer heat of Srirangapatna, there had been no sign of rain for weeks. The ground was hard, baked by the sun. The skies above held nothing but an unrelenting glare. It was in this dry, parched land that I chose to perform an ancestral ritual—a ritual that I didn't fully understand.

A shaman had seen a rift in my ancestral line and also the opportunity to soothe it now with a peace offering. I did as I was instructed. I had carried with me four miniature swords (the size of keychains), a pink rose sapling, and immeasurable hope. The swords were heavy with meaning, forged not of steel but representing soul imprints that were ready to be rewritten.

I stepped onto the earth, tools in hand, and began digging. The land resisted at first. The soil was stubborn, dry. My palms blistered as I worked. I had chosen this spot with intention—a quiet space not far from the Kaveri, where no one would interrupt me. Just me, the heat, and the old ghosts I was finally laying to rest.

I placed the swords into the hole and offered flowers and water. I covered it with some mud and then, on top of this layer, I planted the pink rose sapling. Not a fiery red rose—that would have signalled passion. Not white, which would have meant detachment. But pink, the colour of soft love. Self-love. Healing love. A gentle kind of power.

And just as I was about to cover the base with soil, something shifted.

It started with a sudden wind. I saw clouds gather with unimaginable speed. I heard thunder that made my insides quiver. At first, large drops of rain fell with great force. The skies, which had been bone-dry all day, opened. A full summer rain exploded within seconds in the middle of a drought.

I stood still for a moment, stunned. Soaking in this blessing that seemed terrifying at first but was unmistakably sacred. I felt goosebumps rise despite the heat. I could sense something ancient watching me and nodding.

I whispered a few words—not loud, not for anyone else—and stood up.

The swords were gone. The rose had taken their place.

And just as I stood, preparing to let the ritual settle into stillness—they came.

A group of goats appeared out of nowhere, rushing towards the freshly planted rose. Before I could react, they devoured the soft new leaves, tore at the stem, and trampled the soil I had so carefully laid. The rose was gone in moments. Eaten. Uprooted. Erased.

I froze. It felt like a cruel joke, a violation. I had done everything right—chosen the symbol, set the intention, buried the past—and now this?

It wasn't the ritual I had imagined. It wasn't pretty. But it was real. Maybe the rose wasn't meant to stay. Maybe its brief presence was enough. The ritual wasn't about preservation. It was about release.

The rose may have been eaten. But the swords were buried. And the skies—those dry, unyielding skies—had wept with me.

Rituals often don't work the way we expect—and neither does healing. Just like that eaten rose, our efforts may seem wasted. But something beneath the surface always shifts.

We may not understand rituals and may even mock them if they don't fit our comprehension, which is constantly seeking evidence and for everything to add up neatly. Life rarely adds up neatly.

A young woman once asked me: 'He was the one who hurt me. And now I have to go through the pain and heal. How did it become my fault that he was mentally ill?'

It is unfortunate, but no matter what anyone else does or doesn't do to us, healing is our primary responsibility. If we don't take it up actively, we cause more harm to the body and mind. Worse, we start hurting others in the same way we were hurt.

How Unprocessed Emotions Create Emotional Blockages

Imagine a river flowing freely. When a storm hits, debris falls into the water, and over time, if not cleared, these obstructions create blockages. The same happens with emotions. If sadness, anger, or betrayal are not fully acknowledged, they don't vanish—they accumulate.

Unprocessed emotions manifest in diverse ways. A woman who never grieved her father's abandonment might unconsciously push away romantic partners, fearing rejection before it even happens. A man who was constantly told to 'be strong' as a child might struggle to express vulnerability in adulthood, leading to superficial relationships and chronic loneliness.

These blockages are rarely conscious. They often show up in unexpected ways: digestive issues, tension in the shoulders, or the inability to move forward in life despite external success.

Physician and trauma expert Gabor Maté's work highlights how emotional repression can lead to physical illness. The stress of unresolved emotions taxes the nervous system, keeping the body in a constant low-grade fight-or-flight response. Over time, this can manifest as autoimmune disorders, chronic pain, or even cardiovascular disease. Healing is not just about the mind; it is about the whole being. This is where rituals come in.

The Fire Ritual of Release: Luv and Kush in Valmiki's Ashram

Indian mythology is rich with stories of healing and transformation through rituals. One such account is the fire ceremony performed by Sage Valmiki for Sita's twin sons, Luv and Kush. This ritual marked their shift from princes of Ayodhya to seekers of dharma in the forest. It demonstrates the power of fire as a tool for release and renewal.

After Sita left the palace of Ayodhya, she found refuge in Sage Valmiki's ashram. There, she raised her sons away from royal life, choosing the simplicity and discipline of forest living. Though they were the sons of Rama, they lived without recognition or privilege.

At an appropriate time, Sage Valmiki performed a fire ceremony (*agni kunda yajna*) for the young boys. In ancient India, fire rituals were often used to mark significant life transitions, and this was such a moment. Through the ritual, Valmiki intended to release the boys from the burdens of their lineage and to guide them towards their own path of dharma.

The sacrificial fire (agni) was lit in the centre of the ashram. Sita, Luv, and Kush sat quietly before the fire as Valmiki prepared the offerings. In Vedic tradition, fire is both witness and purifier. It consumes offerings and transforms them into spiritual merit, carrying prayers to the divine.

Valmiki addressed the boys. 'This fire is here to transform,' he said. 'Through it, we release what no longer serves us, and we invoke what we wish to become.'

Luv and Kush each held small bundles of twigs, symbolising the inner burdens they were ready to release. Valmiki instructed them to speak aloud what they wished to let go of, offering it into the flames.

Luv stepped forward first. He said, 'I release my longing for a father I have never known. I release the sorrow of what might have been.' He placed his offering in the fire. The flames rose, accepting the release.

Kush followed. 'I release my anger at fate. I release the name of Prince, for today I become a student of dharma.'

He, too, placed his bundle into the fire, and again the flames consumed it.

This ritual was not only about letting go, as Valmiki reminded them that one must also declare a new intention. 'The emptiness created by release must be filled with purpose,' he said. 'What do you now seek to become?'

Luv closed his eyes. 'I seek endurance, not as a warrior, but in life.'

Kush said, 'I seek wisdom, not from kings, but from the forest.'

Their words became offerings, carried by the fire to the gods. Sita then came forward. In her hands was a simple garland made of wildflowers from the forest where they now lived. Without words, she placed it into the fire. After a silent moment, she spoke quietly. 'May this fire protect them and bear witness to their truth.'

The ritual concluded as the fire burned steadily, its energy transformed. Valmiki placed his hands on the heads of Luv and Kush. 'You are no longer who you were. Remember this.'

In that moment, something shifted. The ceremony was not just symbolic. It enacted an inner transformation. Luv and Kush stepped away from the fire feeling lighter, unburdened, and ready for a new life.

This story illustrates the ancient belief in the power of ritual to mark inner change. Fire, as purifier and witness, is central to many Vedic practices. It helps release attachments, acknowledge loss, and create space for new intentions.

The fire ceremony at Valmiki's ashram was not a grand event. It was simple but profound. It marked a transition that allowed Luv and Kush to move from their past into their future.

Such rituals remain relevant today. Whether lighting a lamp or offering symbolic burdens into a fire, we continue to seek moments where we can let go and transform. Fire becomes not only a symbol of destruction but of renewal and possibility.

I perform fire ceremonies often to calm and heal. Apart from fire, I have found the forest to be a great facilitator of health, balance, and restoration. In fact, I wrote this book while staying in the thick of the Western Ghats at a time when I was going through much healing.

I was woken up by the lilting sounds of the blue whistling thrush every morning. I ate lunch by a stream. I could feel the jumping water's sounds plucking the unwanted energy from me and releasing it into the air. I would go on long evening walks deep inside the woods with the setting Sun and sunbirds for company. The forest has secrets at every turn. If we surrender to her, she can heal us.

But it works only if we are ready for the healing. While nature is a fantastic healer—arguably the best of them all—only when we surrender to her charms do we transform. Going to a beachside retreat when still stiff and not yet soft enough for the change can be a wasted trip. For this reason, it's important to time our rendezvous with nature, too, especially if healing is on the mind.

WHY ACTIVE HEALING IS IMPORTANT

Let's begin by looking at the difference between active healing and passive 'healing'. A self-explanatory suggestion would be that active healing involves doing things consciously to heal, while passive healing means that we trust time to do the healing. That's quite right.

A popular adage goes that time heals all wounds. It says that even if we did something or not, we would still heal over time. But this is an incorrect, or rather incomplete, suggestion. No doubt, time is an essential ingredient in the healing process. It could be the healing of a physical wound or an emotional hurt. Healing takes time, surely. But just as we use medication or antidotes and serums to heal physical wounds, we also need tools to heal our emotional and energetic intrusions.

Healing is not simply the passage of time. If it were, we would all wake up one day, suddenly unburdened by the past. But anyone who has experienced heartbreak knows that pain lingers. It settles in the body, in the mind, and in the small spaces of our everyday lives. The truth is: Healing is not just something that happens to us; it is something we participate in. This is the difference between passive healing and active healing.

Passive healing is the process of simply waiting for emotions to fade, hoping that time will take care of the wounds. It is the belief that if we distract ourselves long enough, if we stay busy enough, if we suppress the pain deep enough, one day it will be gone. Passive healing looks like avoidance—avoiding the memories, avoiding the grief, avoiding the depth of what the relationship meant. It is surviving, not thriving.

Active healing, on the other hand, is a conscious decision to engage with our pain in a way that allows transformation. It is not about dwelling on heartbreak but about acknowledging it, working with it, and ultimately releasing it. Active healing looks like creating space to grieve, allowing emotions to move through us instead of burying them. It means seeking out rituals, practices, or conversations that help us process what happened. It is taking a step forward, even when we do not feel ready.

Rituals are a powerful tool in active healing because they provide a tangible way to release what no longer serves us. Whether it is writing a letter we never send, burning old memories in a fire, or immersing ourselves in a sacred practice, these acts signal to our subconscious that we are ready to let go. They create movement where there was once stagnation. They allow us to participate in our own healing, rather than waiting for life to do it for us.

Passive healing leaves us at the mercy of time, hoping that distance alone will bring peace. Active healing empowers us to create that peace, to take ownership of our healing process, and to step into the next chapter of our lives with intention. The pain may not disappear overnight, but every action we take in healing is a step towards freedom. And that is what truly transforms us.

Healing is not a straight line; it is a spiral. Healing also integrates both active and passive journeys. Passive healing feels as though we are not doing much, but the intelligent human body is at work all the time, relentlessly so. It is always working in our favour. We must give it its due.

While active healing can push us forward, there are times when we must allow space for passive healing to integrate our efforts. Letting go of the pressure to heal does not mean giving up; it means trusting that the work we have already done continues to unfold in ways we cannot always see. This looks starkly different from not doing any work at all or drawing no awareness to it.

Healing is not about forcing an end to pain but about allowing it to dissolve layer by layer. Sometimes, stepping back is also a step forward. The key is knowing when to engage and when to rest, understanding that both are part of the journey towards wholeness.

The Psychological and Physiological Benefits of Rituals

Rituals have existed in every culture for a reason. They provide structure when we feel lost. They externalise what is internal, giving form to the formless. Beyond their symbolic nature, however, rituals have tangible psychological and physiological effects. Research shows that repetitive, intentional actions can calm the nervous system and reduce stress. For instance, Karl & Fischer (2020) found that participants who performed habitual religious rituals experienced significantly greater reductions in both self-reported and physiological anxiety compared to those who didn't perform rituals. This aligns with the idea that a simple nightly ritual—like lighting a candle to acknowledge grief—can act as a subtle signal to the body that it is safe, helping to lower stress responses.

Consider a mother who has lost a child. Each year, on the child's birthday, she lights a lamp and offers flowers at their favourite spot. This ritual does not bring the child back, but it gives her grief a place to exist, preventing it from being locked away and festering into something heavier. The act itself is soothing—it allows her to feel, to acknowledge, and to heal in increments.

Similarly, movement-based rituals such as yoga or dance help release stored emotions from the body. Trauma therapist Peter Levine notes that animals naturally shake after experiencing fear, thereby releasing stress from the nervous system. Humans, however, often suppress these impulses. Dance, breathwork, or even conscious shaking can support the release of trapped emotions, allowing us to process what words cannot.

Why Symbolic Actions Help Integrate Emotions

Rituals work because they engage both the conscious and subconscious mind. On a cognitive level, they provide closure and create a sense of control in situations where we feel powerless. Spiritually, they connect us to something greater, whether it is the collective human experience, nature, or the divine.

Take, for example, a fire ritual where someone writes down old resentments, burns them, and watches the smoke rise. This action tells the subconscious, 'I am releasing this.' Even if we logically know that writing something on paper does not erase the past, the symbolic act bridges the internal and external world, making the process of letting go more real.

Another example is water rituals. In many traditions, people immerse themselves in rivers or oceans to cleanse not just the body but the soul. The act of submerging in water and emerging anew mirrors the internal process of emotional rebirth. Whether through the Ganges in India, the baptismal waters in Christianity, or even the simple act of taking a mindful shower, water-based rituals help us transition from one state of being to another.

The key to any ritual is not just the act itself but the intention behind it. When we approach a ritual with presence, we allow ourselves to engage fully with our emotions, to release what no longer serves us, and to integrate the lessons of our experiences. Healing is not a passive process, but neither is it something that can be forced. It is a dance between action and surrender, between effort and trust. And rituals, whether grand or simple, help us find that balance.

Different Rituals for the Release of Stuck Emotions and Heartbreak

Healing from heartbreak and emotional pain requires more than just time—it requires intentional release. Rituals provide a powerful way to process and release stuck emotions, offering both symbolic and physiological relief.

Here are some rituals that you can try. Most don't need supervision, but if a healer can facilitate the ritual, it can be done in a sacred space in ceremony. That, too, is part of the ritual.

Fire Rituals (Burning Letters, Candle Meditations)

Fire has long been associated with transformation and the burning away of karma. Writing down emotions, memories, or the names of people we need to release, and then burning the paper, allows us to externalise the pain and witness it dissolve.

In animist cultures, homa or fire ceremonies hold great significance as tools for manifestation, transformation, healing, and release.

Candle meditations, in which you focus on a flame while setting an intention to let go, help cultivate inner clarity and closure.

Water Rituals (Releasing Offerings into a River, Bathing as Purification)

Water represents renewal and emotional cleansing. Water is life itself. Even drinking water that is considered holy can cleanse us if we believe.

Releasing flower petals, leaves, or dissolvable paper with written emotions into a river or ocean helps carry away old wounds.

Ritual baths with herbs, salt, or essential oils can wash away stagnant energy, leaving you feeling lighter.

Standing under the rain or immersing yourself in a body of water with the intention of letting go can be incredibly cathartic.

Writing and Storytelling as Cathartic Release

We are made up of stories. Stories define us and allow us to live different realities in the most creative ways possible.

Journalling is one of the simplest and most effective rituals. Writing about emotions without censoring allows the subconscious mind to process pain.

Writing a letter to someone—whether you send it or not—can bring clarity and emotional closure.

Turning pain into poetry, stories, or art externalises emotions, making them easier to process and release.

Movement-Based Rituals (Dance, Yoga, Shaking)

Trauma and emotions are stored in the body. Studies show that in restricted environments (such as corporate offices), employees move in ways that reflect their state of mind. Movement can be limited, leaving the full range of the human body's capabilities unexplored. Intentional movement can help release stuck energy in the body.

Dance and free movement help shake off residual grief and stress.

Yoga, especially heart-opening postures, facilitates emotional release while grounding the body.

Shaking, an instinctive response to trauma observed in animals, is a practice used in somatic healing to discharge pent-up emotions.

Sound Healing (Mantras, Chanting, Music)

Sound vibrations influence our nervous system. Sound, when delivered at certain frequencies, can move through us in unimaginably healing ways.

Chanting mantras or affirmations shifts emotional states and clears stuck energy.

Playing or listening to specific frequencies, such as those from singing bowls or binaural beats, helps realign emotional balance.

Vocalising emotions—through singing, humming, or even screaming into a pillow—can be a powerful way to release pain.

Ancestral Healing or Karmic Release Ceremonies

Some emotions we carry are not solely ours; they are inherited. Ancestral energies have been with us since the time we were born. Our choices in this life give us opportunities to release some of those burdens if they are holding us back from growth. At the same time, ancestral gifts empower us to move beyond our potential and flourish.

Vedic rituals such as Amavasya Tarpanam and Pitru Paksha rites honour and release ancestral pain. They hold the power to break generational cycles of trauma.

Lighting a candle or offering prayers to ancestors with the intention of releasing inherited wounds can bring profound healing.

Participating in guided karmic release ceremonies helps one let go of past-life or ancestral burdens that influence present struggles. An example is Systemic Family Constellations therapy, which combines group work with ritualistic resolution.

Each of these practices offers a distinct pathway to emotional release. The key is to choose the one that resonates most, and to approach it with intention, presence, and an open heart.

HOW TO CHOOSE THE RIGHT RITUAL FOR YOU

Choosing the right ritual for emotional release is a deeply personal process. There is no single method or universal remedy that works for everyone—what matters most is finding an approach that resonates with your emotional needs, personal beliefs, and natural tendencies at that moment in your life.

The first step is self-awareness. Ask yourself: How do I naturally process emotions? Do I need physical movement to release pent-up energy, or do I find comfort in stillness and reflection?

If you feel emotions in the body as tightness, heaviness, or restlessness, movement-based rituals such as dance, yoga, or shaking can be effective.

If you process emotions through thoughts and words, journalling, storytelling, or chanting may be more helpful.

If you feel a strong need for external cleansing, water-based rituals such as bathing or immersing in a river can bring relief.

Many people use a combination of these practices at different times, depending on what they need. If you are unsure where to start, simply begin somewhere—the first step itself matters.

Rituals are most powerful when they align with your personal or cultural beliefs. If you have a spiritual practice, weaving in elements of that tradition can make a ritual more meaningful.

If you do not follow any particular tradition, you can still create rituals that feel sacred to you—for instance, lighting a candle with intention, writing your feelings, and burying them in the earth, or simply sitting in stillness.

Experimenting with Different Methods

Healing is not a one-size-fits-all process. What works at one stage of your journey may not work at another. It is important to experiment and notice how your body and mind respond each time.

Try a fire ritual one week, a water-based ritual the next, and observe which brings the deepest sense of release. Pay attention to how you feel before, during, and after each practice.

Creating a Personalised Ritual

Intuition is a powerful guide in choosing the right ritual. Instead of rigidly following prescribed methods, adapt them to suit your needs.

If a particular place feels significant (such as a park, temple, or corner of your home), use that space for your ritual.

Combining elements can also be powerful: for example, writing emotions on paper (air), burning them (fire), and washing your hands afterwards (water) to symbolise full release.

Integrating the Release

A ritual is not just an isolated event—it marks the beginning of a shift. What we do with intention afterwards helps the desired energy carry through. A closing or integrating element is just as important as the ritual itself. To anchor the effects, consider the following:

a. **Daily reminders:** Keep a small object from the ritual (such as a stone, candle, or written affirmation) to remind you of your commitment to healing.

b. **Journalling reflections:** Record how the ritual made you feel and note any changes you observe in the following days.

c. **Ongoing self-care:** Support the release with continued self-care—through meditation, movement, or simply allowing emotions to surface.

d. **Trust the process:** Healing is not always immediate. Sometimes, the effects unfold gradually. Trust that each step you take is guiding you towards emotional freedom.

Choosing and integrating a ritual is about creating space for transformation after heartbreak or trauma. When done with intention, these practices become more than symbolic—they become stepping stones towards a lighter, freer self.

13

Relying on the Body's Wisdom: Moving to Heal

Swatee went through much of her childhood with an overpowering elder sister who imposed her thoughts and will on the younger one. The home environment was agonising for Swatee, with parents who avoided addressing the issue of dominance with their firstborn, as they didn't want to invite her wrath. Too young to defend herself, Swatee grew up not knowing how to assert herself. With only the bare minimum survival skills and no way to escape her oppressors, she adopted a few coping mechanisms. One was perfection; the other was people-pleasing.

She believed that if only she did a little more for them, they would understand her; then they would finally love her in the way she deserved. But that day never came, even as she relentlessly kept striving to please them.

Swatee went to therapy and gave herself the gift of healing. She came to understand the archetypes and the not-so-uncommon story she had been an unwilling player in. She decided to claim her power and free herself from the trap of toxic family dynamics.

A powerful move such as this is never easy. Swatee had to work hard to repair her body, mind, emotions, and energy. When she began the work with a brave face, her body signalled its protest through the discomfort that often comes with change.

When she stood up to her sister for the first time, her sister perceived it as a direct affront and revolted as though she were going to lift the Sun itself and hurl it out of the solar system. The rage threatened to consume Swatee completely. But she had thought this through and even expected it. She had to set a new boundary, and that was never easy. Still, she persisted.

The stress of this huge transformation—possibly the greatest Swatee would ever experience—brought on persistent digestive issues. One day her stomach felt bloated; the next she had cramps; and the third she was constipated. There always seemed to be some problem or another with her digestion. Friends told her it was because of overwork and constantly eating out. That could be true. But had Swatee slowed down to connect with her emotions, she might have realised it was also a case of the gut–brain axis going awry, as unresolved emotions tied to her relationships kept surfacing in the form of digestive distress.

Swatee believed she had managed the issue and 'closed it' by drawing a fierce boundary. But what about the unresolved hurt, the feelings of inadequacy, and all the harm already inflicted on her? Those feelings had nowhere to go, so they settled within the body, became stuck, and prevented it from functioning freely.

After a major relationship breakdown, it's common to experience loss of appetite, nausea, stomach cramps, bloating, constipation, or diarrhoea. Stress and grief can trigger irritable bowel syndrome (IBS) or worsen pre-existing digestive conditions. Swatee experienced all these symptoms.

She would have benefited by heeding her body's message. The insight was there, if only she leaned in to listen. But it is also common to rush to tackle the immediate discomfort rather than the root cause of the problem.

Swatee's experience is not uncommon. Many of us think we've 'moved on' and are done with a story simply because we've convinced our minds to stop dwelling on an old wound. But the body often tells a different story. Unprocessed emotions don't vanish—they sink deeper into our systems. The body becomes a quiet storehouse, holding grief in the lungs, heartbreak in the chest, and fear in the belly. Over time, what is unexpressed gets compressed. And what gets compressed eventually creates blockages, pain, and illness.

The Body as an Emotional Storage System

When we go through any kind of trauma, it's rarely just emotional—it's physical. You can feel the tightness in your chest, like a weight pressing on your ribcage. Or your stomach feels knotted, tense, or even completely shut down, refusing food or reacting badly to it. Then there's the exhaustion—a fatigue that rest doesn't always cure. Your sleep becomes irregular: Some nights you can't close your eyes; other nights you sleep too much because life feels too heavy to carry awake.

This is the body doing its job: holding, storing, and carrying unresolved emotions until we are ready to release them. The body isn't the enemy here. It's the container, and sometimes the compass, pointing us towards the emotions we haven't faced yet.

Swatee had convinced herself that her life was full—even joyful in many ways—but the cramps and bloating told her otherwise. They were symptoms, yes, but they were also signals. Her body was trying to speak to her in the only language it knew—physical discomfort.

Distraction Is Not Listening

Most of us don't listen. Not because we don't want to, but because we're conditioned to keep moving. We fill our days with work, endless scrolling on social media, over-scheduling, or even over-exercising, believing that if we keep going, the pain will dissolve on its own. Swatee had done this too, busying herself with work and friends. But all the activity in the world couldn't drown out the messages her body was sending.

Distraction is a temporary balm. But eventually, the body raises its voice.

The Body Knows How to Heal: The Story of Rishi Mandavya

There are many Indian mythological stories that speak of using the body to heal. This one appears in the Adi Parva, the first book of the epic Mahabharata.

Long ago, in a quiet forest on the outskirts of a kingdom, lived Rishi Mandavya. He was a sage renowned not only for his profound meditations but for his unwavering stillness. Day after day, he sat in silence at the doorway of his small hermitage, exploring the vast inner worlds of consciousness. His body was his temple, a vessel he understood deeply, and through it he accessed the mysteries of life.

But one day, his body would become his greatest teacher.

It began when a band of thieves, fleeing after robbing the king's treasury, took refuge near Mandavya's hermitage. When the king's soldiers arrived in pursuit, they found only the rishi, seated motionless in meditation. They mistook his silence for guilt and accused him of harbouring the criminals. Without trial or compassion, the king ordered a brutal punishment: Mandavya was to be impaled on a sharpened stake.

Any ordinary man would have perished from the shock and pain. But Mandavya was not ordinary. As the wooden stake pierced his body, he did not resist. He did not fight the pain. Instead, he turned his awareness inward. He listened to his body, not as an enemy to be conquered but as an ally to be understood.

Mandavya noticed something profound in that moment of excruciating pain. The more he resisted, the sharper the suffering became. But as he softened his breath, released tension, and surrendered, something shifted. His body, even in agony, held a quiet intelligence. It knew how to survive. It knew how to heal. He slowed his breathing, guiding his life force (prana) to the places that hurt most. He observed the rhythm of his heart, calming it, reducing the flow of blood from his wounds. Every sensation became part of his meditation—not an interruption, but a teacher.

Days passed, yet Mandavya did not die. His body, rather than collapsing under torture, began to adapt. His pain was excruciating but it no longer consumed him. Instead, it became energy he learnt to work with. He discovered that pain, when faced with awareness instead of fear, could be transformed. The body, when honoured rather than punished, held the power not just to endure but to transcend.

When the king realised the enormity of his mistake, he ordered Mandavya's release. But by then, the stake had fused into his flesh. Even when they carefully removed it, a fragment remained lodged deep within him. Most would have seen this as a wound that would never heal. But Mandavya saw it differently. He did not treat it as a scar to be erased but as a reminder of the body's wisdom. His pain became his meditation; his wound became his guru.

Over time, Mandavya's practice deepened. His body, once a source of suffering, became a gateway to higher states of awareness. He taught his disciples that the body is not a prison of flesh and bone—it is a sacred guide. If we listen closely enough, it will show us how to heal.

Later in his life, Mandavya sought out Yama, the God of Death. 'Why did I, an innocent man, suffer such cruelty?' he asked. Yama replied that in childhood, Mandavya had once harmed an insect, and this was the karma of that action.

But the sage, now wise from his suffering, saw the injustice of punishing a child for unconscious acts. His experience had taught him compassion—not just for himself but for all beings. He declared a new cosmic law: No child under twelve would bear the burden of karmic retribution. His pain had shaped him into a being of higher understanding, capable of rewriting cosmic laws.

Mandavya's life became a living teaching: healing is not about erasing the wound but integrating it. The body holds our greatest wisdom—it knows how to survive, how to restore balance, and how to guide us back to wholeness. In times of heartbreak and loss, when the mind is loud and restless, the body quietly calls us home. If we listen, as Mandavya did, it will show us the way.

WHAT HAPPENS WHEN WE IGNORE THE BODY

Gabor Maté, in his book *When the Body Says No*, discusses how emotional repression can lead to chronic illness. He describes how people who habitually suppress their emotions—especially anger, grief, and sadness—are more prone to physical ailments such as autoimmune diseases, chronic fatigue, and even cancer.

Maté explains that unprocessed emotional pain doesn't disappear; it simply finds novel places to live in the body. When we ignore these signals, we end up carrying unresolved hurt as chronic anxiety, permanent muscle tension, or deeper physical illness. His work reminds us that emotional honesty isn't simply good for the soul—it's vital for physical health.

Swatee's digestive issues were a warning sign. Had she continued ignoring them, they might have developed into a chronic illness. If she had learnt to listen sooner, she could have begun the process of release and healing much earlier. But we start when we are ready to start, and only when we truly understand the importance of listening to the body's wisdom.

Listening to the Body's Wisdom

How do we do this? How do we begin to hear what the body has to say?

1. Body Scans

A simple practice is a daily body scan. Sit quietly, close your eyes, and bring your attention to each part of your body. Start at your toes and move up slowly. Notice: Where do you feel tightness? Where is the heat? Where is there numbness? These sensations are messages, asking for your awareness.

2. Locating Emotions in the Body

Different emotions often live in different places. Grief can sit heavy in the lungs, heartbreak can ache in the heart, and fear can curl itself into the stomach. When you feel something, ask: Where in my body do I feel this? And what happens when I breathe into that space? Sometimes, simply noticing and bringing attention to that area softens it a little.

3. Stillness vs Movement

Listening to the body doesn't always mean being still. Sometimes it means movement—gentle stretching, dancing, yoga, or simply shaking out the tension. At other times, it calls for rest and stillness, doing nothing but lying down and breathing. The key is to ask: What does my body need right now? And then honour that need, whether it's stillness or motion.

This requires experimentation before you can truly discern your body's needs. Those needs may also change depending on the situation or the day. Some days call for stillness, while others call for movement. The practice lies in listening to what your body needs in that moment and tending to it with care.

Swatee's journey could have begun earlier had she listened. Yet her readiness to listen also played a crucial role. Sometimes we know what is required but remain unwilling to submit to the often-difficult path.

Like Rishi Mandavya, who transformed his physical suffering into spiritual awakening by listening deeply to his body, we, too, can turn towards our own physical experiences—not with fear, but with curiosity and care.

Our bodies are always speaking. The question is: are we ready to listen?

THE BODY AS A TOOL FOR EMOTIONAL HEALING AND GROWTH

Heartbreak is not just a story we tell ourselves. It's a *felt* experience. It settles in the body—in your muscles, your gut, your breath. Healing from heartbreak, then, isn't something that happens *only* in your thoughts. It's not just a mental process of understanding why it happened, assigning blame, or even forgiving. True healing requires re-integrating the body.

For many people, this is a new concept. We're so used to thinking about pain, analysing it, and trying to 'figure it out'. But the body has its own language. It's always speaking—often louder than the mind—if we take a moment to listen.

The Body Has Always Been a Spiritual Tool

Across spiritual traditions—whether in India, China, Mexico, or other indigenous cultures—the body has always been seen as a vessel for transformation. Our ancestors knew that healing and spiritual evolution couldn't happen in the mind alone.

1. Movement-Based Practices

Yoga is the most familiar example for many of us. It was never meant to be just an exercise routine. It was designed to align the physical body so that the energy body—prana—could move freely. Each pose works not only on flexibility or strength but also on emotional release. Backbends open the heart space; hip openers release stuck grief and anger.

Similarly, dance has been used for centuries as a way to express and release emotions. Whether it's the classical dances of India or tribal dances from Africa, movement helps us process emotions too big for words. Even martial arts such as Kalaripayattu or Tai Chi are about moving energy through the body in a conscious, deliberate way. And something as simple as *walking meditation*—a slow, intentional walk with full awareness of each step and breath—can bring us back into our bodies after heartbreak has left us feeling disconnected.

2. Breathwork

Breath is the bridge between the body and mind. When you're anxious or heartbroken, your breath becomes shallow and erratic. You hold your breath without realising it. But if you take conscious control of your breath, you can shift your emotional state. Practices such as pranayama, box breathing, or simply placing your hand on your heart and breathing slowly can calm the nervous system.

Many traditions use breath to *release* emotions. Some modern breathwork sessions go deep into catharsis—people laugh, cry, or shout simply from breathing in a particular rhythm. Breathing helps move stuck emotions, especially after heartbreak.

3. Fasting and Physical Discipline

Fasting is often misunderstood as punishment. However, in many spiritual traditions, it's a way of quieting the noise of the body so we can listen to its deeper wisdom. When we fast—whether from food, technology, or unnecessary conversations—we begin to hear our inner voice more clearly.

Physical disciplines such as *vrat* (spiritual vows), *maun* (silence), or long pilgrimages were designed to build resilience, discipline, and clarity—not just physically, but emotionally. For someone healing from a break-up, taking on a gentle, self-imposed discipline (a morning walk, a no-complaining vow, a digital detox) can shift emotional energy in profound ways.

What Modern Science Says

Bessel van der Kolk, one of the foremost trauma researchers, speaks of this in his book *The Body Keeps the Score*. His work shows that trauma isn't just memory stored in the brain—it leaves a physical imprint on the body. Emotional pain, grief, and betrayal aren't just fleeting feelings. They leave the nervous system in a state of high alert, constantly waiting for the next blow. This is why heartbreak often makes us feel frozen. Stuck. Unable to move forward, no matter how much we *think* about it. Our nervous system gets caught in a stress loop—fight, flight, or freeze—and doesn't know how to break free.

Van der Kolk advocates somatic healing, which involves the entire body, not just the mind. Yoga, shaking, deep breathing, and dance—all of these help reset the nervous system. They gently release trauma stored in muscles, posture, and breath.

For instance, someone going through a painful break-up might find themselves emotionally numb, unable to cry or feel joy. They may not even notice they're holding their breath. But when they begin practising yoga—even gentle, restorative postures—or they dance for just five minutes a day, something shifts. Tears come unexpectedly. Laughter, too. The body starts to *feel* again. Healing, in this way, becomes a full-body experience.

Talking Isn't Enough

One of the biggest takeaways from Van der Kolk's work—and what Rishi Mandavya's story reminds us—is that healing requires more than *talking about* pain. It's not that therapy or conversations with friends aren't helpful. They are. But we also need to bring the body into the conversation.

When heartbreak happens, we often try to reason our way out of it. We analyse; we rationalise. But the truth is, the heart doesn't heal through logic. It heals through movement, breath, stillness, and being.

Your Body Wants to Heal

Here's the most hopeful part: Your body already knows how to heal. It's wired for it. Your breath will naturally slow down if you let it. Your muscles will soften if you give them permission. The body isn't against you—it's on your side, always. Sometimes we just have to get out of our heads and give the body space to do what it knows.

Swatee, from the earlier story, only began to heal when she reconnected with her physical body. She learnt this through a Vipassana meditation course. Simply sitting in stillness for a few minutes every day with her body gave her more insights than a full body check-up and diagnosis ever could. The small act of paying attention to her body, saying: *I'm here. I'm listening,* was all that was needed. And that's when healing began.

How to Reconnect with Your Body after Heartbreak

When heartbreak happens, many of us go straight to our heads. We overthink, overanalyse, and try to make sense of it all. But healing is not just an intellectual process. If the mind is busy trying to solve the problem, the body is quietly holding on to the pain.

Coming back to the body is essential. It's the doorway to feeling whole again. But how do you do it? Here are simple, practical ways to reconnect with your body after heartbreak.

Understand Your Personal Emotional Patterns

The first step is understanding *how* you naturally process emotions. Not everyone heals the same way. Some people need movement to release energy through the body. Others need stillness and quiet to process emotions. Some express their feelings best through creative outlets like writing or art.

Ask yourself:

- Do I feel better after moving my body—like going for a walk, dancing, or running?
- Or do I feel calmer when I sit still—through meditation, journalling, or quiet reflection?

- Do I need to talk it out with someone? Or do I prefer silent time with myself?

There is no right or wrong. The key is to notice what soothes you versus what overwhelms you. For me, too much social activity drains me even in normal situations. When I'm emotionally overwhelmed, I need even more space and time to heal. I also use a combination of movement and stillness. But I prefer gentle movements rather than anything rigorous or excessive like high-energy dancing. It could be the opposite for you. The key is to learn the language of your body.

Tuning into the Body's Rhythms

Your body has its own natural rhythms. Emotions aren't constant; they rise and fall like waves. Some days you'll feel light, other days, heavy. Healing isn't linear.

Start noticing:

- When do you feel more emotional—morning, evening, or late at night?
- Do your energy levels drop at certain times?
- Are there triggers—places, songs, or conversations—that tighten your chest or make you tense?

By observing your body's patterns, you'll start moving *with* your emotions rather than fighting against them.

For example, if you feel heavy in the evening, plan something soothing. Light a candle, take a bath, or listen to calming music. If mornings are tough, start your day with movement or fresh air.

Small, Daily Practices to Stay Connected

Healing doesn't happen all at once. Small, regular acts of care build trust with your body and gradually restore balance. Here are simple things you can do every day:

a. **Hand on heart**: Pause for a minute. Place your hand over your heart. Feel the warmth of your hand and the beat of your heart. Breathe slowly. This tells your body: *I'm here. I'm safe.*

b. **Notice your posture**: Check in with your shoulders, jaw, and belly. Are they tight? Soften them. Let your body relax as often as you remember.

c. **Physical touch**: Hug a pillow or wrap yourself in a blanket. Try self-massage—press into your feet or rub your arms gently. Touch reminds the nervous system that comfort is available.

d. **Movement or stillness**: Depending on how you feel, take a walk or sit quietly for a few minutes. Tune in and ask your body what it needs.

Reconnecting with your body after heartbreak is like learning to trust again. The body may have carried your pain, but it also carries your healing. When you listen, soften, and move gently with its signals, you begin to come home to yourself.

Integrating the Release: Making Body Awareness a Habit

Healing from heartbreak isn't a single event but a continuous practice. Even after you've completed a ritual or found relief through movement or breath, emotions can return in waves. This is natural. What matters is how you stay connected to yourself through those moments.

The body is always speaking. Each day, take a moment to check in: *What do I feel? What does my body need right now?* Some days it might need stillness and rest; on others, it may call for movement or expression. As you become more attuned, you'll notice when old emotional wounds show up as physical tension, fatigue, or unease. When that happens, respond with kindness. Breathe deeply. Move gently. Listen. This is the path of integration, which turns body awareness into an everyday habit. It's not about perfection but about presence. Over time, working with your body allows you to release emotions as they arise, rather than letting them build up and weigh you down.

Your body doesn't just hold the pain of heartbreak; it holds the wisdom to heal it. When you partner with your body, heartbreak becomes more than loss. It becomes a doorway to deeper self-awareness, resilience, and growth.

14

Opening Your Heart Again: From Self-Love to New Love

A beautiful embodiment of living through love is Grandma Droniak. I stumbled across her Instagram profile a few years ago, and I've been quietly cheering for her ever since. The 95-year-young, sprightly woman has become a beacon of joy and resilience to her 3.6 million followers, offering playful but deeply grounded advice on dating, heartbreak, and how to keep living it up no matter what age you are. She leads by example, not just in what she says, but in how she moves through life.

Her videos are a masterclass in self-love and joy. She makes GRWM (Get Ready with Me) videos, sitting at her vanity as she holds up earrings shaped like lemons or little rabbits, debating which ones to wear. She'll match them with a bright sweater, swipe on a little lipstick, and do her makeup in front of the camera. There's an ease and delight in these small choices—a gentle reminder that how we adorn ourselves can be an act of love. Then, with a playful wink, she heads out on her date. Later, she returns and tells us how it went—sometimes with a shrug, sometimes with a chuckle, but always with honesty.

There's no pretence with her. She tells her young, smitten followers without hesitation: 'Dump the guy.' Especially if he isn't treating you well. Her message is clear—don't waste time where you aren't valued. You deserve more, at any age. It's not about cynicism; it's about self-respect. And somehow, when she says it, it feels like the most compassionate advice in the world delivered in the most deadpan manner.

Grandma Droniak also talks about death often—not in a morbid way, but with a matter-of-fact grace. She attends the funerals of friends. She acknowledges that death hovers nearby, as it always has. But she refuses to be ruled by it. She talks about it the way some people talk about the weather. She knows it's part of the rhythm of things, but in the meantime, she has a life to live.

She recently broke a hip and was told by the doctor that she cannot walk again. Eight months later, she showed us a video of her walking with the help of a stick. Her message? Never trust a man!

She laughs about the dates that don't work out and shows us how to let a man down gently when he's not the right fit. She meets men at the senior home where she lives. She flirts, dances, and shares stories. Her zest for life is rare and heartwarming, like catching a sudden warm breeze on a chilly day.

What I love most about her is that she's still looking for the perfect love, but she refuses to settle. She's complete in herself. She doesn't *need* a man to feel whole—but she's open to sharing her life with someone if they treat her right. She knows exactly who she is. She knows what she brings to the table. And she isn't afraid to eat alone.

There's wisdom in that kind of openness. It's not passive; it's brave. Grandma Droniak shows us that you can carry your history, your wounds, your memories—and still leave space in your heart for something new. She shows us that love isn't about youth or perfection. It's about living fully, loving wisely, and knowing your worth.

And really, what more could any of us ask for?

In so many ways, she reminds me of the kings and queens in our old stories—people who have lived lifetimes in a single lifetime. People who have lost, loved again, and continued walking forward without closing the door to what might come next. Life cycles through joy and loss, through union and separation, but she stays open to the next turn of the wheel.

The Quiet Return of Love

When we think of Gandhari, most of us hold a single image in our minds—one of self-sacrifice. She was the woman who blindfolded herself for life, choosing to give up her sight so she could stand beside her blind husband, Dhritarashtra. This act alone has come to define her in much of our storytelling. Gandhari, the loyal queen. Gandhari, the ascetic. Gandhari, who turned her body into a living penance.

We are taught to see her as the epitome of steadfast love. In many ways, she was. But what happens after that love story ends? After Dhritarashtra's death, after the war that took nearly everything from her, Gandhari was alone. And yet, some lesser-known stories suggest that she found companionship once more. She is said to have lived her final years in the forest, where she found solace in the company of a hermit. A man of quiet wisdom, whose presence brought her comfort and perhaps even love.

This version of Gandhari might seem at odds with what we know of her. How could the woman who blindfolded herself out of devotion to one man, who bore the weight of her family's destruction, open her heart again? We struggle to reconcile these two images—the Gandhari of youthful sacrifice and the Gandhari of later companionship.

And yet, this is the deeper truth of life and love. Hearts are vast, capable of holding multitudes. The love we carry for one person doesn't negate the possibility of loving another. There is no betrayal in beginning again. In fact, throughout Indian mythology, we find many such stories of second love—of people who, after great loss or sorrow, allowed themselves to love again. Not because they forgot their first love, but because life asked them to live on.

One such story is that of Raja Bhoj.

Raja Bhoj and Padmavati: Love Returns Softly

In one of the folklore oral retellings of the story of Raja Bhoj, the wise and noble king was known for his learning and justice. His first wife, whose name has been lost in many tellings, was the love of his early life. She was his companion in youth and in the building of his kingdom. Together, they created a life rooted in dharma and mutual respect. When she passed away, Bhoj was heartbroken. He ruled his kingdom with fairness, but his heart had grown quiet, as if a great stillness had settled there.

For many years, he remained alone, living with his grief. But life, as it often does, brought change in unexpected ways. One day, Raja Bhoj heard of a woman named Padmavati (from Kuntala), a princess of great intellect and kindness. Their meeting was not one of fiery passion, but of mutual understanding. She, too, had known loss. They found in each other gentle companionship.

Raja Bhoj married Padmavati. Yet he never forgot his first queen. In his private temple, he kept a small oil lamp burning in memory of his first wife. Every evening, he would pause and offer a silent prayer for her soul. His marriage to Padmavati did not erase his earlier love; instead, it made space for both. Padmavati understood this. Together, they built a life that was not about replacement, but about renewal.

King Vikram and Amrita: The Second Bloom

A famous folklore story of the courageous King Vikram states that he loved his queen deeply. Her death marked a turning point in his life. He immersed himself in his duties, governance, and spiritual reflection. Many believed he had given up on love entirely, that his heart had closed its doors for good.

But years later, while on a pilgrimage, Vikram met Amrita. She was not a queen, nor was she born into royalty. She was a simple woman who lived by the river, tending to pilgrims and offering food and water to those who passed by. There was a quiet dignity in her, a grace that needed no adornment. In her presence, Vikram found the peace he hadn't known for years.

Their love was not grand or marked by royal ceremony. It was humble, like the drawing of water from a well on a balmy day. Necessary. Life-giving. Vikram married Amrita in a simple ceremony by the riverside. She brought him companionship in his later years, and with her, he rediscovered the gentle joy of shared silence, of a hand held in twilight.

He still honoured the memory of his first queen. In the palace gardens, he planted a tree in her name, where flowers bloomed each year in her season. But he allowed himself to love again, not in spite of his grief, but alongside it.

These stories remind us that love after loss is not a betrayal. It is a testament to life's ability to renew itself, to offer us companionship and tenderness when we least expect it. Like Gandhari, Bhoj, and Vikram, we may carry old loves in our hearts forever. But that doesn't mean our hearts are closed. They are vast, spacious, and capable of welcoming new love when the time is right.

Cyclical Nature of Time and Love

For those who believe in reincarnation, relationships are teachers. They give us what we need at a particular time, leaving us with lessons we carry forward. All relationships eventually end or transform. They evolve alongside us, shaped by how we engage with them and how we allow them to shape us.

But we often forget the cyclical nature of life. We try to extract everything from our relationships in the short term, focused on immediate gain. One woman may treat love as conquest; another, as validation; yet another, as social currency. Men do the same. When relationships become transactional, their essence disappears behind a silent ledger of give and take.

If we see birth as the beginning, death as the end, and a lifetime as the entire story, we become time-pressed to find the perfect relationship at the perfect moment. It's a cruel expectation to place on ourselves. Life doesn't move in straight lines. It turns in circles—even for those who don't believe in reincarnation. We repeat patterns, meet familiar characters, and walk similar storylines within a single lifetime. Yet we forget this and cling to scraps of connection, afraid love won't return. But magic can happen at any age. Love is a choice we are always free to make.

Not just romantic love. Some of the deepest, most nourishing friendships—even relationships that offer more than romance ever could—can begin at any point in life. Often, bonds forged in later years are more fulfilling and enduring. They rest on foundations of experience, maturity, and, when we're lucky, awareness.

Sometimes we mistake endings for finality when they are only pauses or doorways to what's next. In Indian philosophy, we call this the journey of samskaras—subtle impressions that the soul carries across lifetimes. These imprints draw us towards certain people again and again. Perhaps you've met someone and felt an instant connection, a knowing without explanation. It may be that you have known them before. Some relationships are simply conversations continued from another place and time.

When we understand this, we loosen our grip on control. We no longer need perfect love on a perfect timeline because love isn't bound to a single lifetime. There is always room for return, for unfinished lessons. Love may reappear in another form—a former lover as a friend, a companion as a teacher, or someone new who awakens us to our deepest healing. Life rarely moves in straight lines.

Cycles repeat, not to punish us, but to offer another chance. If we have not fully understood a lesson, life, ever patient, brings us back to it. Sometimes with a different person. Sometimes with the same one, wearing a different face. We find ourselves facing familiar choices until we choose differently. Until we love differently.

And when we do, the cycle completes itself. The pattern dissolves. The wheel turns forward.

In this way, love is less about finding someone new, and more about becoming someone new. Love that returns in our later years often reflects this. After loss, heartbreak, and the release of illusions, we stand clearer in who we are. We no longer seek completion, but companionship. If we have grown in awareness and embody that growth, love meets us there.

This love arrives quietly. It does not chase or cling, nor does it demand proof. It meets us where we are, offering companionship, respect, and understanding.

For some, this love comes after long years of solitude. For others, it arrives in the twilight of life, when society has stopped telling them that romance is possible. And yet, it is often here that love shines its purest light—free of pretence, free of gain.

Indian mythology is rich with such stories. Sages find a deep connection in their final years. Kings and queens marry again, not from duty, but affection. There are reunions—not only between people, but between the soul and its longing for belonging.

If life is a wheel, love is the axis on which it turns. It is never too late. We are never too old, too broken, or too lost. Love finds us, again and again—as teacher, as mirror, as home.

Emotional Landscape of Opening Again

There is a quiet fear that comes with the idea of opening your heart again. It may not be loud or obvious, but it's there—like a door left slightly ajar that you hesitate to push open. After heartbreak, betrayal, or the ending of something you once held sacred, the heart grows cautious. It builds walls, not because it wants to, but because it feels it must.

And yet, somewhere deep inside, there remains a longing. A flicker of curiosity. A softness that refuses to harden completely. This is the beginning of opening your heart again.

However, it's important to honour the emotional journey you will experience. Love doesn't simply reappear. It calls forth old wounds to be seen with fresh eyes. You may find yourself unexpectedly revisiting the grief of the past as you move towards something new. It's not a sign that you're stuck. It's part of the landscape.

Sometimes, when a new person comes into our lives, they hold up a mirror. We see the old scars more clearly, not because the new person is causing them, but because this promising connection is inviting us to be present with all of who we are—including the parts we once closed off. This is why opening again can feel tender. You are entering unfamiliar ground while carrying the memories of the old.

One of the most useful things you can do during this time is to practise *staying with yourself*. Create a refuge within where you are both witness and comfort to your own experience. You don't have to rush to trust someone new. But you can practise trusting yourself again; trusting that you will make choices that honour your heart, that you can be discerning without being closed, and that you are worthy of a love that feels safe.

Be patient with the process. Some days you may feel expansive, ready to embrace new possibilities. Other days, you might feel your heart shrink back, reluctant, and unsure. Both are natural. The rhythm of opening isn't linear; it's a spiral. You will revisit familiar emotions, viewing them from different angles. Over time, what once felt heavy will feel lighter.

There is also the matter of boundaries—soft but clear. They are not walls to keep love out, but gentle fences to protect the garden of your heart as it begins to bloom again. It's okay to take your time. It's okay to say no. It's also okay to say yes, slowly, when it feels right.

And remember, opening your heart again doesn't only happen in romance. It happens in friendships that nourish you, in conversations that make you feel seen, in the simple act of allowing someone to be kind to you without suspicion. Each of these moments is an act of courage. Each one is a step towards love.

The emotional landscape of opening again is vast. It requires courage, tenderness, and a deep trust that life—when you are ready—will meet you with grace.

What It Takes to Open Your Heart Again

Opening your heart again after heartbreak isn't a single decision—it's a slow unfolding. It's not about finding the next person to fill a space, but about reclaiming your own fullness first. The journey back to love begins quietly, within yourself, long before anyone else arrives.

The first step is to become a safe place for your own heart. After loss or disappointment, we often learn to protect ourselves by shutting down. We stop trusting our feelings, or we second-guess our ability to choose well.

But reopening your heart doesn't mean throwing it wide open without discernment. It means listening to yourself with gentleness. You begin by noticing your emotions without judgement—whether that's fear, hope, loneliness, or desire. You give them space. You let them move through you like waves, knowing they don't have to define you. This is the work of self-trust.

Subsequently, the work of self-love becomes the foundation for any future love. Self-love isn't a state of perfection or endless positivity. It's an active relationship you build with yourself every day. And as with any relationship, there are good days and bad days, even with self-love. It is an evolving entity, one that benefits from regular feeding and watering. It's in the small choices—how you speak to yourself, how you care for your body, how you honour your own boundaries—that you begin to show yourself love again. You stop abandoning yourself. You become the partner you long for.

And when you feel grounded in yourself, love flows more naturally outward. But it's important not to rush this. Sometimes we look for new love as a way to distract from pain, hoping that someone else will heal the wounds we haven't fully tended to ourselves. This kind of distraction relies on the memories (apparent and suppressed) of the old love.

True love, the kind that brings nourishment instead of depletion, requires us to be whole enough on our own. Not perfect. Not healed beyond scars. Just present, and willing to meet another from a place of fullness rather than need.

Practical steps can help with this. Spend time doing things that light you up, even if they seem small—whether it's a creative hobby, a daily walk in nature, or reconnecting with old friends who remind you who you are. These acts rebuild your sense of self outside of a relationship. They remind you that your life is already meaningful, already yours.

When you meet new people, stay connected to yourself. Ask: *How does this person make me feel about myself? Do I feel safe, respected, and seen? Am I compromising parts of myself to fit their world?* Stay curious about your own experience.

Opening your heart again takes patience, but it doesn't have to be heavy. It can be playful and light. Love or friendship doesn't always enter with grand declarations—it can arrive quietly, in trust built over time.

And when it does, you'll know. Not because it fills a gap, but because it adds to a life you've already made beautiful on your own.

Pitfalls to Watch Out For

Opening your heart again is a beautiful act of courage, but it can also be complicated. We carry memories, hopes, and wounds from the past. Sometimes, without realising it, we bring old patterns into new spaces. Sometimes, we judge ourselves for still feeling connected to a previous love, even as we welcome someone new. But love, like life, is rarely clean or linear. Here are some gentle reminders and reflections for the journey ahead.

Rushing to Fill a Void

It's easy to mistake loneliness for readiness. There's a difference between wanting companionship and being ready to meet someone from a place of wholeness. Take your time. Let solitude be a companion, not a punishment.

1. Idealising the New Person as a Saviour

No one can heal what you haven't tended to within yourself. A new relationship is not a rescue mission. Be mindful of projecting hopes onto someone instead of seeing them for who they are.

2. Comparing the New with the Old

Sometimes we unconsciously hold up the past relationship as the standard—or warning—for the new one. I once read that in a new relationship, we amplify the one thing that was missing in the old, making it the main condition while minimising the other qualities the new person brings. Every person is different. Stay curious about who's in front of you, rather than measuring them against history.

3. Ignoring Red Flags in the Name of Openness

There's a difference between having an open heart and lacking discernment. An open heart honours both hope and wisdom. Listen to your instincts. Trust yourself to walk away when something doesn't feel right.

How the Old Love Can Coexist with the New

1. Love Doesn't Have to Be Erased to Begin Again

The heart is vast. You don't have to forget the love you once had to welcome something new. There may still be moments when you miss your old love or hold them with tenderness. That's okay. Loving again isn't a betrayal of what was; it's an honouring of how much the heart is capable of loving. What a waste to not let the heart use its full capacity for love and compassion.

2. Grief and Joy Can Walk Together

You may find that even as you feel excitement for a new connection, there's a quiet thread of grief for what didn't last. Both can exist. You're allowed to feel them both. One doesn't cancel the other.

3. Let the Old Teach You, But Let It Not Define You

Every relationship leaves lessons. Take what's useful. Leave what no longer serves you. Your past doesn't have to dictate your future, but it can offer wisdom for how you show up now.

4. Stay Rooted in Your Growth

Who you are now isn't who you were then. Trust that your choices today are made from a deeper, wiser place. Love can return in different forms, but you aren't repeating the same story—unless you choose to.

Opening your heart again is not about replacing the past: It's about expanding into a larger experience of love, one that includes everything you've been through and everything still to come.

Rituals for Inviting New Love

Inviting new love into your life isn't about chasing or forcing. It's about creating space—within yourself and your life—for love to enter naturally. Rituals help us mark that intention in a tangible manner. They give the heart and mind a moment to align, and they remind us that we are co-creators of our experience.

Here are some gentle, simple rituals to invite love in again.

1. Create Space in Your Home

- Look around your physical space. Is it a reflection of the life you want to live with another person?
- Clear out old clutter, especially objects that carry emotional residue from past relationships. You don't have to discard everything but be intentional.
- Leave small invitations: An empty drawer, space at the dining table, an extra toothbrush holder. These subtle gestures signal openness, not desperation.

2. Light a Candle with Intention

- Light a candle in a quiet space, preferably at dawn or dusk—times of transition.
- As the flame flickers, speak softly (or silently) of your readiness to invite love in again. Be honest about where you are—whether it's curious, hesitant, or hopeful.
- Let the candle burn for a few minutes as you sit in stillness. Then blow it out, trusting the intention has been received.

3. Write a Letter to Your Future Love

- Sit with pen and paper, not a screen. Write a letter to the person you are inviting into your life.
- Share your hopes, the life you are building, and what matters to you. You aren't pleading; you're sharing.
- Fold the letter and place it somewhere safe. You can reread it later or leave it as an offering to the universe.

4. Water a Plant with Intention

- Choose a small plant (or a seedling) and make it part of your daily or weekly ritual.
- As you water it, remind yourself: Love, like life, grows with care and patience.
- This practice gently rewires your mind towards nurturing rather than needing.

5. Movement as Prayer

- Dance, stretch, or walk as an offering to your own life force.
- As you move, hold this intention: *I am alive. I am ready for love that honours who I am.*
- Let your body feel free and open. Movement clears stagnant energy and makes room for new experiences.

You Are the Invitation

Love doesn't arrive because we demand it. It arrives because we become an invitation to it. The rituals you practice are not to summon another person, but to remind yourself that you are already whole, already worthy, already enough.

In time, when the cycle turns again, love may find its way to your doorstep. It won't be because you chased it, but because you made space for it with your presence, your joy, and your readiness.

Whether love comes today, tomorrow, or years from now, you have already chosen it by choosing yourself first. And that is the deepest love of all.

15

Rekindling Joy and Love: For You and for Those around You

There is a moment in every heartbreak where we believe love has left us. We sit with the emptiness, convinced that the story is over, that what we lost is final. But love, in its truest form, is not a single story. It is not bound by roles or timelines. It does not live only in romance or partnership. Love is a current, flowing through every chapter of our lives—sometimes as longing, sometimes as service, and sometimes as freedom. When we let it, love can become our purpose.

The river Ganga teaches us this.

Ganga: Love That Flows beyond Loss

In her earthly life, Ganga loved deeply. She was not just the celestial river but also a woman, a mother, a wife. She descended from the heavens to be with King Shantanu, and their love was the kind that reshapes destinies. Yet their story was not without sorrow. Bound by a promise, Ganga took each of their children back to the river, releasing them from earthly life moments after they were born. Only when Bhishma was born did she stay, raising him until it was time for him to return to his father.

After Bhishma was handed over, Ganga left Shantanu. She did not remain to claim a life of comfort or royalty. She returned to her element: She became the river again.

This is often where we leave Ganga's story—as if she left Shantanu and disappeared. But that is not true. She kept flowing. She nurtured fields, quenched the thirst of countless beings, and became a sacred lifeline for civilisations. She continued to give life, even after her personal love story had ended.

Ganga shows us that love does not end when a relationship does. She teaches us that the love we carry can continue flowing into the world, long after the roles we played—wife, mother, beloved—have dissolved. Love is not confined to a person; it is a state of being. And when we choose to stay open, to remain in the flow, we become a vessel for love in its highest, most purposeful form.

Even later, when Bhishma lay dying on the bed of arrows, it was Ganga who came to him—not as his mother alone, but as the sacred river, cleansing, forgiving, and releasing. She did not withhold her love because of what was lost. She gave because love had become her nature.

Chudala and Sikhidwaja: Love as Awakening

Chudala's story, too, speaks of love that transforms and transcends the boundaries of a relationship.

She was a queen—wise, radiant, and deeply spiritual. Her husband, King Sikhidwaja, was devoted to her, but he could not understand the spiritual insights she tried to share. While she found enlightenment within the palace walls, he believed he needed to renounce everything and live in the forest to attain the same. So he left her behind, convinced that worldly life was an obstacle to his spiritual growth.

Chudala did not fall into sorrow or bitterness. She could have lamented that he abandoned their love. She could have closed her heart. But she didn't. Instead, she deepened her own spiritual practice. And when she saw that Sikhidwaja was still lost—still clinging to false notions of renunciation—she chose to guide him.

Disguised as a young ascetic named Kumbha, Chudala met Sikhidwaja in the forest. With patience and compassion, she became his teacher. She taught him that true renunciation is not of the world, but of the ego; that enlightenment is not found in isolation, but in understanding the self, wherever you are. Slowly, Sikhidwaja awakened.

Only then did Chudala reveal herself. She had never truly left him. Instead, she loved him enough to become his guide, to let their love evolve beyond a married couple into guru and disciple.

Chudala's love found its purpose in awakening. She did not see love as possession or permanence. She saw love as a path to help another find freedom.

LOVE AS A LIVING PURPOSE

These stories remind us that love is not a static place we arrive at, a destination we either reach or fail to find. Love is a practice, a current, a living purpose. It evolves as we evolve. Sometimes, love asks us to stay. Sometimes, it asks us to let go. Sometimes, it transforms into service, healing, or wisdom shared.

When we lose a relationship or when love changes form, we can mistakenly believe it is gone. But Ganga teaches us to keep flowing. Chudala teaches us to keep awakening. Love, in its highest form, becomes dharma—a sacred duty to embody compassion, wisdom, and grace, wherever we are.

This chapter is not about finding love as an end goal. It is about becoming love—letting it guide how we live, how we give, how we heal others and ourselves. When love is no longer something we seek, but something we express, we step into a different kind of power: A purpose that lasts far beyond any single relationship.

Love was never meant to be a destination. It was always meant to be a journey.

Love as a Purpose, Not an End Goal

Somewhere along the way, we were told that love was something we had to find, a prize waiting at the end of the road if we worked hard enough, healed enough, or waited long enough. We were taught to imagine love as an arrival point—whether romantic, familial, or a deep friendship—where we could finally rest, finally be whole, finally be complete.

But love was never meant to be an end goal. Love, in its truest essence, is a way of living. It's not something we find; it's something we become.

Love Moves beyond the Self

There's a quiet shift that happens when we stop seeing love as something we need and start seeing it as something we live each day. It moves us beyond the borders of our own longing and into something much greater. The longing itself is not wrong. It's human to want to be seen, held, and chosen. But when we become stuck in waiting—waiting for someone to arrive, waiting for love to prove our worth, waiting for the perfect relationship to validate our existence—we miss the deeper invitation.

Because love, real love, asks us to move beyond the self.

When you have genuinely loved—whether a partner, a child, or a friend—you already know this. You've sacrificed sleep to soothe someone's pain. You've stayed up late listening to their heartbreak, even when your own heart was weary. You've forgiven when it wasn't easy. You've extended grace when you didn't have to. And in those moments, love wasn't just about how it made you feel. It was about what it asked of you. It was about who you became because of it.

That's what gives love its meaning. Not the arrival, not the possession, not even the security of being loved in return. It's who we become when we love. Love transforms us because it demands that we step outside ourselves.

Love with Purpose Leads Us to Service

When love stops being a transaction—'what can I get from this?'—it naturally begins to flow into service, creation, and healing. Not because we are selfless martyrs, but because love, by nature, is abundant. When you love, really love, you have something to give. You *want* to give.

You may have experienced this after heartbreak or loss. At first, the heart closes. It's afraid. But then, slowly, you may notice you're drawn to help someone else heal. You comfort a friend. You create something beautiful. You find yourself wanting to contribute, even in a small way, to someone else's joy. That's love repurposing itself. It's saying, 'I may not be held in the way I imagined, but I can hold someone else.'

Some of the greatest acts of dharma and seva in our stories came from people who once loved deeply and lost. Savitri loved Satyavan fiercely, but after his death, her life did not end with her grief. She created a haven for widows and abandoned women, giving them dignity and hope. Manthara, known from the Ramayana as the maid who manipulated Kaikeyi, found redemption and purpose by raising Luv and Kush, offering them love and guidance in their early years.

Love with a purpose doesn't just heal the self. It becomes a force of healing for the world.

Love Evolves and Expands

One of the most liberating truths about love is that it doesn't have to remain in one form. It isn't frozen in time or locked inside a single relationship. Love evolves as we evolve. It may begin in romance—fiery, consuming, electric—and later soften into quiet companionship or fierce friendship. It may start with one person and ripple outward into a community. It may even shift into love for the divine, for the earth, for life itself.

Ganga didn't stop loving when she left Shantanu. Her love transformed. She became the river that nourished all beings. Chudala didn't stop loving Sikhidwaja when he left her behind in search of enlightenment. She became his guide and his guru. Love didn't die. It evolved.

We forget this when we grieve the ending of a love story. We think it's over because the form has changed. But love doesn't die. It asks to be reborn in another way—sometimes in friendship with the same person, sometimes in mothering ourselves, sometimes in guiding others through their darkness because we've known our own.

The question is not, 'Is there love in my life?' It's, 'What form is love asking to take now?'

Seeking Love as an End vs Becoming Love as a Practice

When we seek love as an end goal, we attach it to an outcome. We tell ourselves, 'When I find love, then I'll be happy. Then I'll be healed. Then I'll be whole.' Love becomes something to acquire, like a possession we earn if we are good enough or lucky enough. In this limiting form, love becomes conditional, bound by rules of how it must appear, how it is expressed, what it is, and who should receive it.

But when we become love as a practice, everything changes. We stop waiting. We start being. We embody love in how we speak, how we listen, and how we offer ourselves to the world. Love becomes the way we move through life, not a destination we are desperate to reach.

You may already be practising this without realising it:

- The way you water your plants and greet the sunrise.
- The way you comfort a stranger or forgive someone who hurt you.
- The way you cook your meals or write words that heal.
- The way you sit quietly with yourself and offer compassion to the parts of you still learning to trust.

These acts of love may not be grand, but they matter. They matter because they bring love into the world as an energy, a frequency, not just a role or a label.

And when you live this way, something softens. You no longer live in scarcity, measuring whether love is 'enough' in your life. You realise you *are* love. You are enough.

Love as a Teacher, Love as a Journey

In the end, love isn't something we get to keep. We get to experience it, learn from it, be shaped by it, and when the time comes, we have to allow it to transform us. But it doesn't belong to us. It moves through us. And if we are lucky, if we are wise, we let it keep moving.

When we understand this, we are never without love. It becomes like breathing. Even when we are alone, we are never empty. We are the river that keeps flowing. We are the guide who shows the way. We are the hands that heal, the words that soothe, the presence that comforts.

We need to understand that love isn't the destination. Love is the way home.

HOW TO REKINDLE JOY

Joy doesn't always return on its own after a difficult transition. Sometimes, after heartbreak, loss, or long periods of numbness, we have to invite it back in consciously. Joy can be shy like that. It waits for us to open the door.

Rekindling joy is not about forcing ourselves to 'be happy' or pretending everything is fine. It's about creating small windows where light can enter again. And from those windows, warmth returns—first to you, then to the people around you.

Here are simple, practical ways to rekindle joy in yourself and share that joy with others. Start small. Let the momentum build slowly.

1. Start with Small Moments of Pleasure

When we've been through pain, we often grow accustomed to living in survival mode. We forget what it feels like to experience ease, lightness, or pleasure.

Try this: Make a list of tiny things that feel good. Not massive things like taking a holiday or buying something expensive. Tiny things such as: Drinking chai in the sun, listening to songs from your childhood, smelling fresh flowers or essential oils, wrapping yourself in a soft shawl. Each day, choose one thing from your list and give it your full attention. Let it become a simple ritual. No multitasking. Just you and the moment.

Pleasure in small doses slowly awakens joy. It reminds you that life can feel good again.

2. Move Your Body (Gently, with Kindness)

Joy is a physical experience before it becomes an emotional one. You can't think your way back into joy—you have to move your way back.

Try this: Do five minutes of movement you enjoy. Dance to one song. Stretch on your yoga mat. Walk barefoot on the grass. Choose something that feels good in your body, not something punishing or exhausting. Smile while you move, even if it feels silly. The brain connects physical movement with emotional release. Do this daily if you can, even for just a few minutes.

Joy gets unstuck when the body is no longer frozen in tension.

3. Create Beauty around You

When we beautify our surroundings, we send ourselves a message: Life is worth showing up for. Beauty heals.

Try this: Clear one small space in your home—a corner, a shelf, a table—and make it beautiful. Place flowers, candles, sacred objects, or anything that makes you feel calm and happy. Light a diya every evening and sit beside it in silence for a few minutes. Play soft music in the background during your daily activities. Wear colours that lift your mood. Even if no one sees you, you will.

When your environment feels warm and alive, joy finds it easier to enter.

4. Practise the 3 Rs: Rest, Reflection, Ritual

If you are exhausted, joy can't enter. Tiredness blocks it. We need rest—not just sleep, but deep, nourishing rest.

Try this: Rest – Allow yourself time to do nothing. Take guilt-free naps. Sit by the window without scrolling on your phone. Rest your eyes, your mind, and your heart.

Reflection – Keep a gentle journal. Ask yourself at the end of the day: *What gave me joy today, even a little? What drained my joy today? What do I need to feel more alive tomorrow?*

Ritual – Create a simple ritual that signals a fresh start. Morning tea at sunrise, lighting incense before work, or ending the day with gratitude.

These rituals anchor you in presence. Presence makes space for joy.

5. Give without Expecting Anything Back

One of the quickest ways to feel joy is to give it away. Not because you should, but because generosity creates energy.

Try this: Send a kind message to someone without waiting for a reply. Give a genuine compliment to a stranger. Offer to help in small ways—carry someone's bag, open a door, listen without interrupting. Cook a meal for someone who could use a little care. Pay for someone's chai or snack without them knowing.

These small acts of kindness restore our belief in life's goodness. And that belief is the seed of joy.

6. Create Togetherness, Not Loneliness

Isolation kills joy. We don't have to be surrounded by people all the time, but meaningful connection nourishes us.

Try this: Invite a friend over for tea, with no agenda. Plan a 'shared silence' walk where you walk side by side without needing to talk. Organise a small circle where people can share what's bringing them joy—or what's making it hard to find joy. Make a phone call instead of sending a text. Hear someone's voice. Laugh aloud.

Joy multiplies when it's shared. Even quiet togetherness helps rekindle the spark.

7. Do Something New (However Small)

Stagnation steals joy. Our minds and hearts need freshness to feel alive again.

Try this: Learn a new skill, however small. It could be a recipe, a craft, or a simple meditation technique. Visit a place in your town you've never been before—a park, a bookshop, a temple. Rearrange your space. Move the bed. Shift the furniture. Try writing with your non-dominant hand for fun. Listen to a genre of music you wouldn't normally choose.

Newness wakes us from within. It stirs curiosity. Curiosity leads to wonder. And wonder is the root of joy.

8. Gratitude as a Daily Practice (Even When It's Hard)

You've heard this before, but here's a simpler way to do it—one that isn't overwhelming.

Try this: Every night, write down one thing you're grateful for. Just one. Make it specific, like, 'I'm grateful for the sunlight on my face when I woke up,' 'I'm grateful for the taste of warm food at lunch.'

Sit with the feeling for a few moments before closing your journal.

Gratitude isn't a list—it's a feeling. And it turns the ordinary into something sacred.

9. Invite Playfulness

Joy is playful, yet as adults, we often forget how to play. It isn't childish. It's life-giving.

Try this: Doodle without worrying about how it looks. Dance without choreography. Play board games with friends or family. Tell silly stories or jokes. Skip stones across a lake or blow bubbles in the air.

These small moments of play remind your inner child that life isn't always serious.

10. Make Peace with Where You Are

Sometimes joy hides because we're too busy fighting what is. Making peace doesn't mean giving up—it means softening.

Try this: Sit quietly with your hand over your heart. Breathe in and say (silently or aloud), 'I am where I need to be,' 'I trust joy will find me again.' Speak gently to yourself. Stop rushing your healing or forcing joy to arrive on demand.

Joy returns in its own time. But we can create space for it, and trust that we are never abandoned.

Joy as a Gift We Can Give

When you rekindle joy in yourself, it naturally spills over to those around you. Your energy shifts. Your presence feels lighter. You laugh more easily and listen more openly. You love without grasping.

Rekindling joy isn't selfish. It's the opposite. When you light your own lamp, you help others find their way as well.

Remember:

- Joy doesn't have to be huge.
- It doesn't need to be perfect.
- It only needs to be true.

Start where you are and let joy grow.

A RITUAL TO FIND THE LOVE NO ONE CAN TAKE AWAY

At the heart of this journey lies a simple truth: The love you seek outside has always lived inside you. It is not fragile. It does not depend on anyone's presence or absence. It is not diminished by heartbreak or time. It has been there since the beginning, and it will remain unchanged and untouched.

This ritual is a way to reconnect with that deep, untouchable love—the wellspring of love that is always yours. Here's when and where to do this ritual:

- Choose a quiet time when you won't be disturbed. Early morning or just before bed works beautifully.
- Find a comfortable, clean space where you feel safe. You might sit by a window, at your altar, or in nature.
- Light a candle or a diya if it feels right. The flame represents the light of love within you. Soft music or silence—choose what supports your peace.

Step-by-Step Ritual: Reconnecting with Inner Love

1. Prepare Your Space

Sit comfortably with your spine upright. You may sit cross-legged or in a chair. Rest your hands on your lap, palms open and relaxed.

2. Breathe Into Your Heart

Close your eyes gently. Take three deep breaths. With each exhale, release tension. Bring your awareness to your heart centre. Imagine you are breathing in and out of your heart.

3. Place Your Hands on Your Heart

Now, place both hands over your heart. Feel its rhythm. Silently or softly say: 'I am here. I am home.'

4. Visualise the Inner Flame

Imagine a small golden light inside your chest. See it glowing softly, like a steady flame. This is your love. It is ancient. It has witnessed everything you've been through and remained pure.

5. Let the Light Grow

With each breath, see this light grow larger. It fills your chest and your body, then radiates beyond you. You are surrounded by the warmth of your own love.

6. Receive and Give Love

As you sit in this light, feel it nourishing you. Whisper to yourself: 'I am loved. I am love itself.' Imagine this love touching every part of you—especially the parts that have felt abandoned, broken, or lonely.

Then, if you feel ready, send a small stream of this love outward—to the people you love, to those who've hurt you, and to the world.

7. Close the Ritual with Gratitude

After 10–15 minutes, bring your hands together in a prayer position. Thank yourself for showing up. Thank the love within you for being patient and constant. Blow out the candle (if you lit one), knowing the flame inside you never goes out.

8. Repeat Regularly

You can do this ritual whenever you feel disconnected, unloved, or lonely. It reminds you that your deepest source of love is never outside you.

LOVE AS A PURPOSE: LIVING BEYOND THE SELF

Many of us begin the journey with love as an end goal—wanting to be loved, searching for 'the one', or hoping a relationship will complete us. But love is not a destination you arrive at. It's a way of walking through life. It's a practice. A presence. A purpose.

When love has a purpose, it doesn't shrink to one person or one relationship. It expands. It becomes the reason you wake up, the energy behind your work, the care you offer others, the peace you bring to your home.

How to Give Purpose to Your Love

Start by asking yourself:

What does love move me to do?
How can I make someone's life lighter, even in small ways?
What is love asking me to create, heal, or serve?

Love with purpose is active. It becomes dharma. It becomes a service. Not necessarily grand acts—but small, meaningful choices every day.

Ways to Live Love as Purpose

Living love as your purpose isn't an abstract ideal—it's a conscious practice woven into everyday life.

One way to embody this is by cultivating compassion, both for yourself and for others. When you act from compassion, your choices naturally reflect love, even in moments of challenge.

Forgiveness is another powerful expression. Whether you're forgiving yourself for past choices or releasing the pain others have caused, forgiveness frees your heart, making more space for love to flow through you.

Service is yet another path. Offering your time, energy, or presence in service to others—without expectation—aligns you with the deeper currents of love.

Creativity can also be an expression of love's purpose. Whether through art, music, writing, or simply the way you prepare a meal, allowing your creative energy to flow is love made manifest.

Finally, living with authenticity—showing up as your true self, even when it's hard—is one of the purest ways to honour love as your life's purpose. When you choose to be real, you invite others to do the same, creating a ripple of genuine connection.

How to Identify Your Purpose

Identifying your purpose isn't about finding a single, grand mission that defines your life. It's about tuning in to what makes your heart feel alive and what brings you deep fulfilment.

Begin by reflecting on what you love doing so much that you lose track of time. These moments of flow often point to your purpose. Pay attention to what people come to you for—whether it's advice, comfort, creativity, or support—as these are usually gifts you offer naturally.

Notice the causes or communities you feel most drawn to support, as they reveal where your heart longs to make a difference. Consider the challenges you've faced; often, our deepest wounds lead us to our most meaningful work. Lastly, listen to your intuition. Your inner voice, when quiet enough to hear, whispers the truth of your purpose long before the mind catches up. Trust it. You're not here by accident.

Love Is the Journey

When love becomes your purpose, you stop chasing it. You start being it. You no longer wait for someone to complete you. You are complete in yourself and overflowing. You become the river, not the cup. And in that flow, you heal yourself and those around you.

Every act of love—towards yourself, another, or the world—creates meaning. It gives you a reason to wake up and live fully. And this kind of love never ends.

May you awaken it and experience its beauty.

Afterword

The Journey Continues

When I first sat down to draft this book, I thought I was writing about heartbreak. But now, as I close these pages, I've come to see I've been writing about love all along.

Not the kind of love that comes and goes, not the one we wait for or lose sleep over. But the love that is already here. The love that lives quietly beneath the noise of the world—the one you carry in your own breath, your own body, your own being.

You may have picked up this book in a moment of loss, or longing, or quiet curiosity—or even hope. But if there's one thing I hope you take away, it's this: Love was never outside of you. It was never waiting at some far-off destination. It has always been waiting for you to come home to it.

I have walked this road, too. I have sat in the silence after the goodbye. I have stood at the doorway of a new beginning, unsure if my heart was strong enough to open again. And what I know now is this—love will meet you exactly where you are. It doesn't demand perfection. It simply asks for your presence.

Heartbreak may have led you here, but this is not the end—it's the beginning of a wider, deeper experience of love.

Love Along the Way

Love will find you. Whether you are looking for it or not. Whether you believe you are ready or not.

It may not arrive in the form you expect. It may not stay in the way you hoped. But love has its own quiet rhythm. It comes in laughter shared with a friend, in the steady companionship of your own breath, in the unexpected tenderness of a stranger's kindness.

And when it comes, it may quietly ask: What will you do with it? You can hold it close for a while or let it pass through you like the wind. You can dance with it for a moment or let it rest silently in your company. You can choose to walk away. Or you can choose to stay. There is no wrong answer.

Because love was never something you had to earn. It was never something you had to chase. It was always something you were.

This journey, whether you are at the beginning or somewhere in the middle, is not about finding the perfect love story. It is about becoming the place where love can land, where it can breathe, where it can stay or go, and be free either way.

This is a turning point. You may close this book, but your story is still unfolding. There will be new days, new conversations, new hands to hold. There will be moments when you feel more whole than you ever thought possible. And there will be moments when you forget everything you've learnt and need to be reminded again. That's all right. We are all remembering and forgetting and remembering again. That, too, is part of love's rhythm.

And as you walk forward from here, love will find you again. In a conversation, in a sunset, in a hand you hold, in a choice you make. It may wear a familiar face. Or it may not.

So, if you do one thing after reading these words, let it be this: Stay open . . .

To the softness that still lives in you.

To the possibility of joy in the smallest moments.

To the truth that you are worthy—not because of who stays or who leaves, but because you are alive and breathing and here.

You are love, and you are loved.

With all my heart,
Sumaa Tekur

Acknowledgements

As I began drafting this book, I was reminded once again what an uphill trek this is. And yet, year after year, the yearning to tell stories keeps me going. This one, in particular, was a challenging book to write—both triggering and cathartic in so many ways. I wrote two earlier versions while trying to match the relentless pace of city life. But eventually, my exasperation seeped into the manuscript, and I was left holding a draft that mirrored the jadedness of what humanity is becoming.

So, I retreated to a rainforest in the South Indian hills of Coorg. Tucked away in the expanse of the Western Ghats, I discovered a 25-acre spice and coffee plantation, Rainforest Retreat, lovingly nurtured by two passionate scientists, Sujata and Anurag, and their beautiful daughter, Maya.

I am deeply grateful to them for opening their doors and allowing me to experience this magical slice of the world. From this vantage point, life felt vast again—like inhaling the universe deeply and exhaling the dust and manipulations of the city.

Here, I healed through every pore of my being, shaking free from the demands of the urban wilderness and its laws of selfishness. I am grateful for the trees that let me witness them—and be witnessed. Grateful to the universe for bringing me here, to meet the sun, the moon, and the stars all over again.

And gratitude, especially, to my daily wake-up call—the Malabar Whistling Thrush, a blue beauty that prefers to be heard rather than seen. She sang me out of my dreams each morning with lilting whistles that no alarm clock could ever rival.

Sujata and Anurag are rare souls. They walked away from the predictability of urban life, the lure of high-paying jobs, and the applause of easy success to create something that plays the sustainable game: A life of harmony with nature. Their work in organic farming and conservation is not a project; it's a pilgrimage. They lead by example—quietly, without fanfare, building a world where ecology and economy coexist without destroying each other. Their passion for the earth is contagious; it leaves you questioning your own choices and inspires you to live a little more gently.

To Sujata, thank you for being the guardian spirit of this forest and of my time here. Your kindness had a pulse; it reached me in ways you may never fully know. And to Maya, Ravi, Muthupande, Lakshmi, Lakshmana, Leela, Vikas, and Pampa—each of you added a note to the symphony of this experience. And then there was Janice—the soulful dog who came visiting every day. In her, I found lessons in love and freedom that no human could have taught me.

You each enriched my insights into relationships by adding a burst of yellow where I saw only grey.

Thank you to Hay House India for continuing to believe in my voice. Sonali, my editor—you are patient, perceptive, and everything a writer hopes for in an editorial partner.

Thank you, Arundhathi, for recognising the heartbeat of this book and sharing your thoughts so generously.

To Prashanth, thank you for being the first reader and critic of this manuscript. And to my circle of truth-tellers: Sairica, my soul sister; Lisa, my empathetic listener—you walked beside me when the path was hardest.

As I leave this forest, I know this: Endings will always come. But they are not the enemy. Here, among trees that shed and bloom in quiet rhythm, I learnt what this book now tries to tell you—every ending, no matter how painful, is an invitation to begin again.